Walter Lecky

Pere Monnier's Ward

a novel

Walter Lecky

Pere Monnier's Ward
a novel

ISBN/EAN: 9783741190063

Manufactured in Europe, USA, Canada, Australia, Japa

Cover: Foto ©Andreas Hilbeck / pixelio.de

Manufactured and distributed by brebook publishing software (www.brebook.com)

Walter Lecky

Pere Monnier's Ward

PÈRE MONNIER'S WARD.

A NOVEL.

BY

WALTER LECKY,

Author of "Mr. Billy Buttons," etc.

NEW YORK, CINCINNATI, CHICAGO:
BENZIGER BROTHERS,

PRINTERS TO THE | PUBLISHERS OF
HOLY APOSTOLIC SEE | BENZIGER'S MAGAZINE

To

My Friends

𝕳𝖊𝖑𝖊𝖓, 𝕭𝖊𝖗𝖓𝖊𝖙𝖙𝖊, 𝖆𝖓𝖉 𝕮𝖍𝖆𝖗𝖑𝖊𝖘 𝕮𝖔𝖑𝖑𝖎𝖓𝖘

at

Okwari Camp.

Gentle breath of yours my sails
Must fill, or else my project fails,
Which was to please."—TEMPEST.

CONTENTS.

CHAPTER I.
A GOLDEN LASS, ... 9

CHAPTER II.
A TRAVELLING SHOW, ... 28

CHAPTER III.
A QUIET NOOK, ... 46

CHAPTER IV.
AN EVENING IDYLL, ... 68

CHAPTER V.
A COUNTRY SCHOOL, ... 93

CHAPTER VI.
A PARTING, ... 112

CHAPTER VII.
WINNING A WAY, ... 128

CHAPTER VIII.
The Last Glimpse of Erin, ... 142

CHAPTER IX.
A Man of Fortune, ... 167

CHAPTER X.
The Voice of the Charmer, ... 199

CHAPTER XI.
Out of the Depths, Light, ... 227

CHAPTER XII.
Disentangling the Ravel, ... 257

CHAPTER XIII.
Mors Janua Vitæ, ... 284

PÈRE MONNIER'S WARD.

CHAPTER I.

A GOLDEN LASS.

It was a beautiful June day, a day full of flowery fragrance, that a thin, sallow little man, with a piece of carpet under his arm, a drum on his back, and a child holding loosely the fingers of his right hand, passed through Malone, their faces set towards the mountains. The child was full of chatter and laughter. All things seemed strange to her. She gave skipping chase to the butterfly, imitated the bee in his drowsy monotone, and tried, with little success, to curl her lips for a mockery of the robin as he sat singing on a swinging maple-bough, cheering his mate in her weary task of incubation.

The wayside flowers, poking their bits of color through the grass, or scaling chinks and crannies with a vesture of beauty, passed heedlessly by the country children, were to her objects of wonder, brightening her big, soft, sunny eyes, and urging her mouth to exclamations of delight.

Not without hesitancy did she pluck the fairest, leaving a void that her heart compassioned with a sigh, then nimbly twining them in her yellow curls, or pinning them on her bosom, covered the petals with a bit of lace.

The mountains, wooded to the top with trees, whose foliage of various shades of green, yet so harmoniously blended, and rising with such perfect symmetry, made her think of the long forest line, extending for miles beyond her vision, as but one mighty tree, amid whose branches gambolled strange animals whose forms bore the mint-mark of her young imagination.

The quiet ripple of the Salmon River, along whose banks the road led, was music to her soul, making it long for quiet and a sleep in the long grass that stoled its boundaries.

In this grass, so soft and cool, her little spare arm as a pillow, the robin and river making music, decked with such beautiful flowers as were woven in her curls or heaved with her breast, she could sleep and dream, perhaps go with a good fairy to his lovely land where there is no toil, only honey, milk, and wine, served in crystal goblets, and candies on platters of gold and silver. There all dresses are silk, and ugliness, which is another name for care, never shows his face. Her dead mother had often told her of fairyland and its strange but to-be-coveted things, strange because of the joys and riches; things which had never entered into the mother's life, and could not be foreseen for the daughter. Poverty they knew, not wearing it loosely as a toga, but tight-pinching. In fairy-tales they came close to riches, closer perchance in dreams begot by these tales.

The cruel city had narrowed her life to a little room by night, and a dingy street, long as her mother's call, by day—a street that had become less and less, to fit her mother's voice, until it had brought her to the window of the dingy room at the foot of an old bedstead, holding a corpse covered with a rough yellow cotton sheet, the gift of a poor but kind human neighbor, whose ideas of the dead were that they should be covered becomingly. The household rags, much worn (even rags have their degrees of dignity), long used as a coverlet, not fitting with the good woman's hereditary ideas on the proper laying out of human shells, were carefully folded and put away, the yellow sheet, her own whole-souled gift, taking their place.

Poverty rightly refuses to throw aside its rags, being conscious of the old saw that a half-loaf is better than no bread.

So the child sat, looking now at the face, pale, thin, sorrow-crushed, yet withal seeming rested, then at the yellow sheet, thinking it moved to her sharp cry of " Mamma ! " and when tired of crying, and escaping sorrow for the moment, looking out of the one good glass pane at her playmates' faces, full of sorrow to show a due regard for the supposed feelings of their little friend. When her gaze was withdrawn they became natural; fought in mimic warfare ; laughed, sang, showed their selfishness. Joy was their life, and the sorrow-masks worn at the window merely proved the facial imitativeness of our race.

Then men came, clumsy and rough, and the mother and the yellow sheet were placed in a box, so small compared with the room, and carried out, placed upon a wagon and quickly driven over the cobblestones.

She remained with the kind neighbor, black thoughts flying through her brain like a flock of home-bound crows, each one cawing his own complaint.

The big, rough men did not care for her mamma, that she read in their faces; but somehow she had one thought, begotten from a long study of the dead face, that men and boxes could not hurt it. She happened to communicate this to the good neighbor, whose heart was bleeding not for the dead but for the living.

Her crude thought was: The dead have no present; the living have; and to take care of the present is a hard job for a tiny motherless child. In her kindness she was praying for another coffin, shaking her head to confirm the truth of the idea that had just come to her: "Children sleep best when close to their mothers."

The child's idea, better cut, jostled hers and for a moment seemed to be but her own. Hardship had dulled her brain. Its action was sluggish. At length she understood, and drawing the child closer whispered: "God's peace. She's with Him. She don't want clothes, food—anything. If you've wanted nothing you know how you'd feel."

"Then she'll be always dead," spoke the child, a chilly feeling speeding the nerves to a tremble.

"No, youngster; you're too young to see through my talk. She's more alive and in better health than you be."

"If she is, then," continued the child, "she will want things. Everything that's alive wants something, else it will die."

"Now, my little curly-head, you're bothering me. I have explained my way, just as I come to see it, and if you have to live on this street for forty years, wanting everything—bed, board, water, air, room—in fact everything—when you come to want nothing (that's up with God) I'm thinking you will have peace enough."

"Nobody to love you; all cold——"

"Hush, child; God will love you. Up there it's all love. Sometimes He sends a bit of it to us here, as He did when He took your mother."

"I saw that bit on her face. I knew it was not death. Then He loves my mother and He will love me."

The woman shook her head. The child's brain was too quick, "cunning" she called it, for her old head.

So they kept by the window looking at the poverty, gaunt and grim, creeping up the dingy street, listening to the far-off strains of an organ grinding out "Home, Sweet Home." Now and then came the merry laugh provoked by the supposed antics of a red-hooded, consumptive monkey.

It was winter. The day was cold and snappy, showing its snap in the way the passers-by struck their hands together and the lively way their feet beat the pavement. Night was coming early, creeping at first like a curtain pulled bit by bit to shut off the light, and then somewhat suddenly, darkening the room.

The child leaned her head wearily on the woman's shoulder, watching the lamplighter light the sputtering gas. Then she began to blink, thinking the snowflakes were armies of white moths courting destruction, and with this thought gentle sleep entered the room, and, indifferent to surroundings, poured on the woe of the child his balm.

The good woman lifted her tenderly and softly laid her on the bed, and gathering the rags, threw them over the sleeping child, folding them in at the ends.

"Now, darling, you won't get cold, even if you have no mother. God look to ye. There's many a one in this big city like you to-night. It would be good for ye that you would never wake. In that sleep bit and board don't trouble us much. It's the only place that poor folks have a chance."

Tears came to the woman's eyes, and visions of her girlhood and country home, buried in her memory cells for years, came trooping, drawing tears and bending her head. Once her life was sweet composure. That was long ago, in the days of maidenhood and beauty, when sorrow had no place in her ideas. The sliding memory told pictures of that time. Then came the lights of the city, so bright, begetting thoughts of snugness and comfort, and she followed, full of belief in them and in herself. Years had come and gone; belief in lights and men had long since fled; sorrow had crushed her life, and a thread held her to hope in the future, a thread often curiously snarled, almost rent in twain, by those who protested so loudly their fulness of belief in that future, yet acted in the present so little in keeping with that belief.

Her musings were banished by a gentle knock, and, as the door was opened, an elderly gentleman bade her a polite " Good-evening."

" I am Mr. Fortune, the owner of these rooms. Is that the woman's child napping there ? Ah, she's dead ! Not much loss. Owes me two months' rent. Not much left to square up. Well, I'm not the first she beat. I'll be a little more shrewd next time. Yes, just a bit more shrewd. I let her stay after the first month was due, and then to spite me she goes off and dies. Well, it's my luck."

The child slept on; the woman eyed him with a vicious look. Such looks rather pleased him. From a beaten dog we demand nothing but snarls.

" Are you anything to the child ? " he asked. " If you are, better take her out of here as soon as you can, in less than an hour. Leave things as you see them. Little enough, you're thinking, to pay two months' rent. I agree with your thoughts."

The woman rose, took the sleeping child on her lap, running the fingers of her right hand through the long yellow curls, matted and tossed, of the little head, as if to give them a more fitting form.

" You won't put us out to-night, will you ? You're a Christian. It's cold and snowing, and the child's sleeping. To-morrow we'll make tracks bright and early. I'll take her then to my home until she gets a better guardian."

"That will afford her little difficulty," said Mr. Fortune, "little ; but you and she must get out quietly, and that before an hour. My house is not the only place that keeps out cold and snow. Better be getting ready. Movement will keep you warm tonight. I will soon return. Hope I won't have any unpleasantness."

The woman neither besought nor asked further mercy. She was, in her own way, a student of human nature. Even animals, from long hunting, instinctively know their enemies.

Another form peered in at the door. The face was prematurely old and furrowed with deep lines of care. There was in it a slight trace of dissipation, yet not enough to spoil a face that once was of more than ordinary beauty. The twinkling eyes had not lost a kindly merriment that nature shot through them.

"Is that you, Sal ? "

"Won't you come in, Charlie, and see the prettiest youngster you ever seen ? " said the woman, rising with her sleeping burden.

"I don't mind if I do," was the cheery response. "I have had always a kind place in my heart for the young. Was once there myself—just once. It's the only land, Sal, you can't get back to. Sit down; I'll find a seat."

He sat on the edge of the bed, while the woman told of Mr. Fortune's demands. Her eyes kept their viciousness; her tears had run dry. He punctuated her tale with a scratchy cough, aided in its chilling effects by a cynical sneer.

The tale was ended. The child awoke looking like a fawn bereft of its mother, muttering that word with that peculiar intonation that clothes deep sorrow.

"Don't speak to me of Fortune. He's neither better nor worse than his gang. A Christian! That's a pretty big name. On that roost you will find quite an assortment of poultry. What use to appeal to him under that flag? His whole life has been passed condemning everything my mother taught the word meant. Yes; I know he's president of a foreign missionary society. The poor devils out there will hear of his virtues; we know the vices. Distance, sure enough, Sal, lends enchantment to the view. To preach and teach is a noble command, but I don't think Christ meant that those at home should be neglected. We hear so much about the slaves abroad. That is to hide those at home. Just see this street with its slaves! Worse than the Zulus! There water and fresh air are free; here you pay for both highly adulterated. Last night I heard Fortune (he wants to get into the Assembly) talk of inalienable rights and patriotism. Fudge, Sal! Yet the slaves laughed. They will send him there, and then he will have a better chance to join other knaves in legislating more slavery. He won't call it by its name; that might make the herd think and stampede. He never went to the front. I did. Some of his relatives get fat pensions for going a few miles. I asked for nothing; don't want anything; did my duty; gave my country a chance to live. That's more than she gives me. But to change the bill, what do you intend to do with the youngster?"

He bent over the child, fumbling in his pocket with one hand for a coin while the other dallied with her curls. As he pressed his only dollar in her hand he kissed her, leaving a shining big tear on her cheeks.

"What a knowing child!" said the woman.

He lifted her in his arms and with his soft musical voice sang her a couplet—

> "Golden lads and lassies all must,
> Like chimney-sweepers, come to dust."

The child seemed comforted and talkative in his arms; the little throbbing heart was relieved by pressing against kindness, and the little eyes saw fortune in the hard-earned, generously given shining dollar.

"Why do you sing me such a sad song?" asked the child, closing his eye with her finger-tip, "why?"

"It is a jolly song, my pretty miss, right jolly, full

of fun. You are too young, but when you are as old as Sal and I, and have been scourged by the world as much, 'come to dust' will be a great relief. Hunted dogs don't look back. There is more peace ahead than behind them. But what shall we do with the golden-headed lass? I wish I was rich, but wishes are too common to be worth anything. Shall Sal take you home?"

The woman arose, paced the room a few times full of thought, and then taking the child in her arms said slowly:

"Rob is at it again. You know what that means. If I took her home he would abuse her. I could never stand that, though she's none of mine. He has been out of work all winter. That has not made him milder. To-day he met some one he knew when he was better off, when we had the store up in the country, and for the sake of old times he treated him. So you see I couldn't bring her in; couldn't. Rob might abuse her. That I couldn't stand. It's hard lines, but Rob is cranky and what can I do? If Mr. Fortune had left us here until the morning, I could have got her a place. You can do something in the daytime."

As they spoke a large van drove to the door, and the driver entered with the news that "he came from Mr. Fortune to gather the things for rent, and wanted the people in the place to clear out before he was done loading, as he had to lock the door and take Mr. Fortune the key."

"There ye are, and Fortune made a speech against the Turks about atrocities. O God, but you suffer a lot of sham in this world!" broke out the woman.

"You see further than I gave you credit for, further, Sal; but I venture to say that the Turk could not be more brutal than the Fortunes. Any way, after such brutality he would not denounce his brothers in crime."

"I want something of my mamma's to take with me," wailed the child.

"Tear off a bit from the rags," said the woman. "It's the only thing that flat-nosed carter will let you have."

"It's near time for youse to be making a start," growled the carter. "This is no weather to be keeping a fellow standing in the cold. I won't shiver much longer at your expense."

"Well, Charlie, kiss your golden lass good-by. You may never see her again," and the kind neighbor wrapped an old shawl about the child, and put an old cap on her head, to fit her for life's first battle.

There were tears in the woman's eyes, tenderness in her voice, a look of anxiety in her face.

"Why, Sal, you don't mean to say that you are going to pass the night in the streets with this child? That would be cruel."

"Where shall I go?" was the quick answer.

"Where? Thank Heaven my rent is paid for two more nights. Here's the key of the room. Perhaps by that time you will see some one who will help. There's nothing to eat, but the dollar will keep you going a day or two, and by that time Luck may give me a sight of her face. If she does you'll see me, with my arms full of good things, perhaps a doll for— what's the child's name, Sal? Genevieve? What a pretty name! A doll, then, for Genevieve, but Genevieve must pray for my luck. My golden lass, here's a kiss. Good-by, Genevieve; and Sal, make yourself comfortable in my fair abode."

He smiled, kissed his hand with the grace of one who had been well-bred, and strode, supperless, roomless, penniless, down the dingy street.

"Who is he?" asked the child, "that good, kind man."

"That, child, is Charles O'Connor, some kind of a newspaper man," said the woman. "Charles O'Connor, and God be with him. He not only gives you his room and walks the street all night, but his last cent. Rob says that he used to be well off afore his wife died; but after that he drank and went to the dogs. He's straightening up now, don't touch a drop; but he's lost his hold, just the same, and can't get anybody to take him. His friends don't want to see him—friends! you don't have any when you're poor—and strangers don't know him. So he's just living on memories more than crumbs. Well, come along. You won't have far to walk. Let that flat-nosed carter hunt for the key; he will have more 'time' to charge Fortune. Come, a bit of a walk will do you good."

They went out into the street. The woman, with her shawl drawn tightly around her face, darted ahead, pulling after her the child, who was curiously peering at all the sights found in the dingy street.

Leaving the street the woman turned into a dark alley-way leading into a squalid court, opened the door of the first house, mounted a rickety, swaying staircase, and turning the key in the door of the first room of the first landing, entered. The room had a bed, small and low-legged, of a pattern long in disuse. A bit of faded carpet, with as many holes as a colander, lay crumpled on the floor. A rough bookshelf, propped with books, held many a precious volume. The walls were covered with old newspapers, evidently put there by way of decoration. There were a few pictures—a cheap copy of Millet's "Angelus," "The Scottish Raid," by Rosa Bonheur, a large and well-executed crayon of a young woman hanging just over his bed, and a few framed photographs of this same woman and a man holding each other's hands.

The child was quick to notice the resemblance in

these photographs to the man who had pressed into her hand the money she now held so firmly. A small table, scattered with newly written pages, an old knife, a bit of india-rubber, a pencil, a pen, two bottles of ink—one black, the other red—and a rickety chair completed the furnishings of the room.

"Dearie, but Charlie's comfortable. It was lucky we met him. I often heard Rob say that when he was in his prime no one went from his door either hungry or thirsty. Rob says he's down for good, but I say, though it's hard to believe it, that every lane has a turn. I hope his will turn soon. Now give me your money and I will go out and buy something to eat. I'll be careful in the spending. Old Sal counts the pennies."

The child held out the dollar, saying, "Buy something for yourself; anything you like, Sal."

The answer was a kiss and a long embrace.

"As it's a bit cold, when I go out you crawl into bed, and be as cosey as a sparrow in its nest. Don't mind sleep, take your fill of it. It's the best thing you can have. I'll wake you up when I come in. I won't be long. I'm going where I can get the most for the money."

She went, and the child prepared for bed, crying a little for mamma. Then, thinking of the kind man and the woman who must have loved him, and how the woman had to go like her mamma and the man remained, all he had of her was the picture above his bed. She wished for her mamma's picture, and, shutting her eyes, saw but a white, worn, dead face and a yellow sheet. Mamma had taught her to pray but one little prayer—"God bless me, and send some work to my mamma." Now that that mamma needed no earthly work the child thought of making a little prayer of her own.

Getting a large book, Webster's Dictionary, she drew it near the bed, knelt upon it, clasped her little hands, shook her golden curls, elevated her eyes, and prayed: "God bless me, and send some work to Charlie and Sal." Then the woman's face caught her eye, and she added: "Make Charlie's lady meet mamma in heaven."

Then she crept into bed, and soft-eyed sleep stole her for awhile from the cares of life.

Sal soon returned with a thin, sallow little man, who bent over the sleeping child, remarking as he did so: "Just the thing; lucky I met you. Better than Jocko. I'll soon teach her pretty tricks."

"So you think she'll do for your business, Parenti. Only I know you for years as a man with a heart as soft as butter, there's no fear that you would get her. If Rob could only get a few days every week, or, for that matter, myself, she would never want a home. But you know how I'm fixed. So you lost Jocko. How was that?"

There were tears in the Italian's eyes as he spoke. "Mrs. Sal, me don't know. She was lively a few hours ago when I was playing near your street. When I come home and went to feed her, she coughed, beat her breast with her paw, then looked at me, and died right off. O Sal, she was company! I brought her from my country, and she made me much money."

"Well, it's too bad, but it might be worse," said the woman, getting a lunch for the child. "Too bad, Parenti. But why should that make you leave the city? Country folks won't care much for your hurdy-gurdy and your antics. You will soon come back."

"No, Sal; I won't come back. I shall do better in the smaller towns, and Veevy," pointing to the child, "will be a great card. I won't burden myself with my hurdy-gurdy, as you call it. I can sell it and get a drum. A few lessons and Veevy can play it. That will call the people; then I can make a speech in Italian (folks like to hear things they don't understand), and I can do tumbling stuff when I have a crowd. Vee—that's the easiest name—can take the pennies. People will give them to her when they would abuse me. After awhile I can teach her a little dancing. Bless Vee's little heart. I shall take as much care of her as I did of Jocko. What I have, she'll have the first bit of it."

"Well, Parenti, I trust you to be kind to her. I'll

wake her up, the sleeping darling, and introduce you. Speak kind to her and don't walk her far at first."

The woman woke the sleeping child with a kiss, and propping her in the bed, made her ready for the repast.

"Child, I've found a father for you, Emil Parenti. You must kiss him and be his good little girl. He will give you nice things. I would like to have you, but what would I do with you? Hard time to keep my own carcass afloat."

"Oh! I will be good, very good; I'll work for you, Sal, if you will keep me," said the child. "Why don't you give me to Charlie? Do leave me here. He said he would be back if he was lucky, and I prayed for that. Won't you, Sal?"

"Come to-morrow, Parenti," said the woman in a husky voice. "The youngster will be in better humor."

He came, and led away a weeping child. They faced to the country. Sal, tear-stained, went forth to seek a day's scrubbing. Charlie had found work, and, happy, returned to claim the little one. His room was empty. He mused long, then sat down to write his "Tales of a Court," the first, "Only a Waif," floating into his mind with memories of the golden lass, Genevieve.

CHAPTER II.

A TRAVELLING SHOW.

Dixon's saw-mill was noted from one end of the Adirondacks to the other. Its proprietor had begun with little, but, by honesty and right treatment of his workmen, he had become known far and wide. His fame brought orders and wealth—wealth gladly welcomed for the use he could make of it in extending his various shops, alleviating the sick, and pensioning all those who had the misfortune to be in any way maimed.

In all his good offices, and they were part of his daily life, his noble wife was his constant adviser.

No inducement, no matter how cunningly devised, could allure a man who had once worked for Dixon to desert him.

Dixon's Mills lay along the Salmon River, deriving their motive power from its stream. The workmen lived near by in neat little cottages, each having in front a bit of courtyard, wherein pretty garden-flowers in summer-time were carefully watched and tended by the happy housewives. The distribution of flower-seed was one of the many offices that fell to the share of Mrs. Dixon. A prize of something useful was given for the best-kept plot. Many a stranger passing through checked his horse more than once to survey the neat cottage and the charming flower-plot. Had the stranger been thoughtful and asked how it was, up in these mountains, that the workmen were clean, thrifty, and full of taste, even the urchin running around the cottage door would have quickly and truthfully answered, " Mr. Dixon, sir."

Such things can one man achieve, even in this selfish age, who practises the two great commandments of the law, loving his God and loving his neighbor.

" Not legislation, but Christianity rightly understood and nobly practised," said Mr. Dixon, " is the true mediator between labor and capital." If his text was disputed, he had not far to go for a living illustration. He could rejoin, " Here I am, capital; there my workmen, labor. Where is the friction ? " " It will come," you answer; " yes, it will come." He would reply, " When I become selfish and love them no longer. Yes; then will it come; no sooner."

The whistle told the cessation of work in Dixon's Mills. A first whistle, a quarter before twelve, was a warning to the women to set their tables and have the steaming dinner ready for their hungry spouses.

" Men," said Mr. Dixon, " think as much of their wives as their wives think of them. Love begets love. A cold dinner destroys the healthy appetency, and shows carelessness which soon breeds discontent. A warm dinner and a good, wifely kiss is a great producer of laughter, which is health. Women should be merry at meal-time. Whining, sour looks, and disagreeable gossip irritate husbands and spoil their dinners. A series of spoiled dinners ends in dyspepsia; then farewell to peace."

One afternoon as the men were returning from dinner they were attracted by the beating of a drum and a childish song.

In front of the mill was a sallow little man, fantastically dressed, grimacing, and, from time to time, feebly gyrating on one foot. By his side was a little blue-eyed, golden-haired girl with flowers woven in her curls and fastened to her breast, beating a drum and singing a plaintive little song about a disconsolate lover that lost his damsel and died of grief.

The workmen, showing signs of welcome in their faces, formed a circle around the strangely mated pair. When the song was ended, the little maiden bowed right courteously, threw a kiss with the tips of her pretty fingers, and made her eyes dance a roguish caprice.

"Bravo!" shouted the men, while they playfully prodded each other and passed pleasant compliments on the charming little play-actress, as they styled her.

Putting down the drum, a load that weighed her to

the ground, she took the clown's hat of her partner, and, with "Mister, if you please?" held it to test the appreciation of her audience, a charming bow, her mode of thanks, for the smallest coin.

"Help her, boys," shouted Mr. Dixon. "She's early in the harness. How snug your children are! This poor waif, once dear to somebody, is now like a bit of drift on the Salmon. Help her, boys! don't be stingy. It's not often we can see a travelling show."

He led off by a silver piece which made the clown smile and bow very low. The workmen, like all contented men of their class, had some money for the fun-makers. They gave with a right good will.

"Sing another song!" shouted somebody.

The clown nodded his head, the child took up her heavy load and beat it violently, and happy was her face.

She sang the same plaintive ditty.

"Something new!" shouted the same somebody.

There was a grin on the clown's face, and tears came to the child's eyes and ran down her face.

"Sing the old song; just keep on, dear," said Mr. Dixon, bending down and kissing the little mouth that puckered to keep in a cry. "Don't mind what that man said. You're young and not long at the business, though long enough, God knows!

Keep on! That's it. Let me hold your drum. Good enough. Good girl."

The child's voice became stronger, the tears fled, and the roguish caprice danced once more in her eyes. The clown unrolled a little bundle of carpet, and spread it on the ground at his leisure. When this was done he delivered a long address in his native tongue, punctuating it with comic gestures and grimaces, which made the children—whose quick ears had heard the first drum-tap, and whose feet soon found whence it came—roar with laughter.

"Boys, he's going to tumble. Widen out, and give him lots of air!" shouted Mr. Dixon. "We'll have the worth of our money."

"What kind of gab is that he's spouting?" said William Cagy, the mail-driver, pulling up his horses to give his passengers a sight at the travelling show.

"That," said Dixon, looking steadily at the clown, "is an Italian. I am banking more on his features than on his 'gab,' as you call it."

Yes, he's colored like them. I guess, Mr. Dixon, you hit it that time," said the stage-driver, dropping his reins and jumping from his coach. His features are pretty well mated to the folk that were working on the new railway last summer. I wonder if he's going on to Squidville? If he is, I'll give him a lift, more for the child's sake than anything else. What a little fairy she is! I would like to steal her; then you fellows would not be joking me with having a nice cage and no bird."

"Let him tumble first, Cagy," shouted a dozen voices, while the children's eyes were full of anger at the man that wished to carry off their travelling show.

"Why don't he go on," said a youngster, "and mind his own business? He's always late! No wonder, if he stops for everything he sees on the road! I wish his horses would run away and break his old coach. That might teach him to sit on his seat and hold his reins."

The child beat her drum and sang her song. The clown tumbled, strutted up and down his piece of carpet, looked through his legs at the laughing crowd, and, in his soft Italian, recited a snatch from some old Italian ballad. The workmen clapped their hands, threw him grimace for grimace, and even tried to imitate his speech. Suddenly he tottered as if drunk. The workmen yelled with delight, shaking their heads and remarking to each other: "He knows all about that; that's the genuine article, as sure as you live!" Then he lay on his back and twisted, uttering low, painful cries.

"What kind of a trick is this he's at?" said one of the lookers-on.

"I'll bet it's something new."

"I don't see much to that," said another.

"Perhaps, if you had to do it, you would think it hard enough," said a third.

The clown tried to rise, but fell back. He pressed his thin, bony hand to his heart and uttered a sharp cry.

The child in a moment was by his side, holding up his head and kissing his mouth.

"You are sick, papa!" It was the first time she had used the word. "Sick—very sick; but you will not die and leave me! Speak to me!"

"The poor fellow is dead," said Mr. Dixon, examining the prostrate man, "quite dead. There is no use in running after a doctor; he could do no good if he was on the spot. When the heart stops ticking there is no clock-maker who can set it a-going. Cleaning and oiling may do while the pendulum wags, but once it stops——"

"Aye, Mr. Dixon," broke in William Cagy, "there's no denying your words. He's a foolish fellow that thinks the spark, once it's out, will burn in the old lamp."

"What shall we do with him?" asked a soft-hearted workman, whose eyes were dim with tears. "He's human, and we can't clay him like a dog. We had better take up a subscription. A little from everybody in the mill will bury him decently. Nobody will miss it. That's an eye-opener. You don't know when your time is up. A few minutes ago he was as lively as a mink, giving good sport; now the hunt is over."

"If we only knew the denomination to which our dead brother belonged," said Mr. Dixon, "we could have him buried with the service of his church. I hope it will never be said of us that a weary brother giving up his load in our town was clayed without that respect which good and bad alike of our race look to as the fitting rounding of life's journey. What we do unto others will be done unto us."

"Pass around the hat," said William Cagy, pulling out his deer-skin bag. "I want to start the ball a-hopping. Make it as big as you can, for the youngster needs a frock, and a few other things."

"Any one who has not money with him," said Mr. Dixon, "may freely borrow from me. There's no excuse; and mind Cagy's advice."

The child clung, weeping and sobbing, to the neck of the dead man, kissing the cold lips, beseeching a word that the wan mouth could never curve.

"Come, come, my dear!" said Mr. Dixon, bending over her. "Your papa is dead. You will sicken yourself with crying."

The child gazed long at the kindly face, and clasped the hands extended to her.

"Does *everybody* die, sir?"

"Yes, my child; everybody, sooner or later."

"I wish I could," continued the child, "and go to mamma and Charlie's lady and God's love. Sal said that was what death is. Don't you see how nice his face is? If Sal was here he would have a sheet. That would make him look nicer. If Charlie was here he would take me, and call me his golden-headed lass. Oh! what shall I do?"

Cagy had crept near the child, and during this recital of her grief showed strongly his emotion.

"What will you do?" he repeated. "Come and be my golden-headed lass. You will have no walking, no drumming. I don't think Mr. Dixon will have any objection to your coming along with me. He knows me a good many years. If you come with me, Mr. Dixon will see that your pa is buried decently. That's all that can be done for him now, if he was a king."

The child arose, and, as if glad of the proffered offer, went to the side of the donor and lifted her eyes to his, seeing there the same light that flashed from the eyes of Charles O'Connor when he pressed her to his bosom and called her his golden-headed lass. That light was kindness—a light which has been the producer of all the little joy men have found in the life-tramp. It sweetened the child's sorrow, and from loneliness evolved hope and friendship.

"Well," said Mr. Dixon, "it is a question if any of us—and the most of us would be glad to do so—have a right to take the child. She may have relatives who will claim her. The best thing would be to have her committed to the poorhouse and then receive legal permission to adopt her. That, William, I believe I could easily procure. You have made the first demand, and the child, in your hands, would have a home such as she has never had. I mention these things, as an ounce of prevention is better than a pound of cure. If you took her, kept her for a year, say, then relatives came along after you became attached, I dare say you would find the parting a difficult matter. Adoption-papers will save all this; so I think the best way is to let the child come to my home for a few days."

"I have no relatives," cried the child. "Mamma is dead, Sal gave me away, and Charlie didn't come back. Then," tugging at Cagy's fingers, "you take me. No one will ever, ever come after me. I shall be very good, take care of your horses, do everything, play the drum for you, if you don't send me to the poorhouse. I heard my mamma pray to God to keep her out of it. Oh, take me! You said you would, and now you are backing out. Try me, and if I am not good, then send me away. Try me, won't you, just once?"

The little maid tried all the teasing airs that nature gives to woman—those airs which constitute her charm—to win the stage-driver's love.

He was not indifferent, if his eyes were a test. He hated poorhouses; the very name jarred his frame.

However, great respect for Mr. Dixon, whose worth and friendship were often attested, restrained him from putting the child into his stage, and, pleased with his luck, driving home. Yet came the thought: "If these papers will take a few days to get in shape, why can't she stay with me as well as with anybody else? I'm sure I can treat her as well as anybody in these parts."

He fell into deep thought.

"Here comes Père Monnier," said a dozen voices.

"It's all in his hands," said Cagy. "He always comes in the nick of time. Whatever he says goes. The child won't go now to the poorhouse, that's one thing sure. Put her in the poorhouse, even for a day, to sting her all her life, and have folks call her *pauper*. And that they would do, for any kind of mud to down you, you will never want flingers. Here's the man that will see through things in a jiffy."

As he communed, a bay pony and light yellow buggy came along and halted by the group of workmen, who touched their hats in respect to the buggy's occupant.

"Good-afternoon, Mr. Dixon. Is it not a little late to be here?"

"Well, yes, Père Monnier, but let one of the men

take your horse, and come here. We have a sad case. It will explain our delay."

The man addressed was tall and active; his form straight as an arrow. He was about forty-three, but so boyish were his features that one could scarcely believe he was out of the twenties.

His hair was long, black, and curly; his eyes a merry blue, with a roguish dash of fun sparkling in them. His features were finely chiselled, which brought him the compliment from young and old that "It would do you good to have a sight of his face."

Beneath the buggy were two of his constant companions, a huge St. Bernard, silent in the crowd, affectionate only to his master, and a pointer, quick, nimble, making friends easily, and forgetting them in a moment, longing to be patted, restless and undignified.

"No need of any one to hold Molly. She won't go unless I'm along, Mr. Dixon. I have only to speak to her and she will be as quiet as a mouse," said Père Monnier, alighting from the buggy, giving place to the pointer, who curled himself in the robe as a safeguard for his master's property.

"Well, you have had a sad affair. The poor man is quite dead, an Italian, a showman; heart-failure, I dare say. This is his little girl—pretty child! Something must be done for her. Do you speak Italian?"

The child negatively nodded her head.

"I don't think she speaks any language but English, Père," said Mr. Dixon.

"I presume you are correct, Mr. Dixon. She is not of foreign extraction. A clean-cut Yankee; shows it in every feature."

"That's the best kind, Père," said Mr. Dixon laughingly, "if it has a chance to develop. I must not go back on my old Vermont stock."

"That's right. Nothing like patriotism. It gives taste to a man, individualizes him," said Père Monnier, opening the dead man's shirt and drawing out a few pieces of tape and a few medals and a crucifix attached, which he reverently withdrew from the man's neck and handed to the child.

"I believe he is of your faith, Père," remarked Mr. Dixon. "And if I am correct we should like to have him buried with all the service that is due to death. We have a sufficient amount to pay all expenses. I am thankful that some good fairy put it in your ear to come our way."

"The fairies are all dead, Mr. Dixon."

"So much the worse, Père, for the world. It seems, nowadays, the thing to make the world as dull as possible. The fairies still live for me."

"And me too," put in one of the workmen.

"No harm," said Père Monnier. "Now as to the dead man. I will readily defray the cost of his burial.

My services are free, and the other little necessaries cost but a trifle. That is all settled."

"No, not in that way," said Mr. Dixon. "Your services we accept, but we, too, must have a hand in the charity. On that I insist."

"Well, be it so," said the priest, "be it so. Mr. Dixon is right. You all claim a share in the good work. But where will he be kept? For it would not be seemly to hasten his burial."

"Leave that to me, Père," said Cagy; "my coop is big enough to harbor the living and the dead. A few days of the tumbler's company won't put me out in the least. I can go around as usual. He doesn't want any care. Yes, leave him to me; no trouble—not a particle—to house for two nights the showman. I can take him along now on the stage, and whenever you're ready you can come for him. Just give me a bit of notice. A piece of paper stuck up in the post-office telling of the sudden take-off of the tumbler, who is a stranger in these parts, and asking all the folks to turn out to the funeral, which starts from William Cagy's, would give him a decent send-off. Jim Weeks could do the writing in a jiffy, and Buttons would only be too glad to plaster it where everybody would drop an eye on to it. I'm waiting for your say, Père."

"I think Cagy's offer a good one," said Mr. Dixon, "but what about the child?" who by this time had found a friend in the big St. Bernard, whose neck her arms encircled. "I suggested to Cagy, who offers to provide her a home, that she ought to be sent to the poorhouse, and then adoption-papers be taken to save all future trouble. I leave the matter entirely in the Père's hands."

"I fear I am a poor judge in such matters," rejoined the priest. "I do not like the poorhouse idea. I have no admiration for such institutions. Children should have love, that requires a soul, and you know institutions of this kind lack that. Even for a few days I am loath to consent. The child has doubtless seen poverty, but it was yoked with love. Let us not introduce her to poverty linked to indifference and selfishness. These two gods rule all such institutions. People argue they are necessary. They may be. Few existing things that cannot find defenders ready with arguments not only to justify their existence but their worth. I don't like them, I am free to say. How could I? I hate their gods. They sour youth and they darken age. I pity those whose miseries have sent them there. For them bitter indeed is the cup of life."

"Yet they are Christian institutions," remarked Mr. Dixon.

"Yes; Christian! What things are done in that name—things the very contrary to its spirit! That name has been a cloak for pagan outrages. Judge its followers, Mr. Dixon, not by their idle, empty pretences, but by their acted lives. Actions, not words, are the test."

"Exactly, Père Monnier," replied Mr. Dixon. "What we need is practical Christianity. The mouth-Christians have brought no end of injury to religion. What do you think is best to do with the child?"

"What I was going to say, Mr. Dixon, was that if Cagy had not the first option on the child, I would take her home and run all risks as to the claims of her relatives. I haven't much fear on that point. They did not care for her much when they allowed her to become part of a travelling show; not but I believe the poor proprietor was kind in his way. A glance can tell that there was no relationship. Where he picked her up and who she is I suppose will never be known, and perhaps it is just as well. Ignorance is oftentimes bliss. The present may be fairer than the past. For this child I hope it will be so. She may have been born amid happiness, sorrow eating it up —who can say? The only witness is dumb. If Cagy had not first say, I would, as I said, take her home to Anna for company. She has already won over one of the pets of our household in Hercules. Other triumphs would follow. The pointer is ready to succumb, while the mastiff, guarding Anna, loves all those that his mistress loves. As to our Napoleon, what a man for children! He always carries candies in his pockets for them."

"Ah, Père! you have given a character to all your household, but the one whom the child will love most is Père Monnier," said Mr. Dixon.

"And does anybody in their senses," said Cagy, "think Cagy so foolish as to take anything from the Père? To tell the truth, if I had got her I would have carried her down some fine night and made her a present to Anna. What would I do with the child? It's too lonesome, my den, for the little girl. Over at the Père's she'll be near enough. It's only a step, and it will give me an excuse to visit. I didn't like the poorhouse talk, so I was a kind of anxious. Now my anxiety is all over. There is a big load off my mind."

He bent down and kissed the child, saying:

"You have now a home fit for a queen; your travelling and poverty are over. Do what Père Monnier tells you and you'll grow up a credit to all belonging to you. You're a lucky little girl, that's all I can say."

"Thank you, William; you shall always have a half-interest in our baby, and you must show your valuation of this interest by calling often," said Père Monnier.

"That I will, Père; and seeing that everything is fixed agreeable to everybody, I make a move we start. I am late with the mail—'the usual thing,' as Buttons says. Well, as I often tell him, news ain't like ripe fruit. A few days' extra boxing won't destroy its taste. Put the tumbler on the stage, boys; set him up, just as if nothing happened to him. Put out his feet a little more, the better to hold his back."

Père Monnier jumped into his buggy, the pointer obligingly clearing the wheel. Mr. Dixon handed him the sobbing child with a tenderness that Père Monnier never forgot. The drum was stored in the box of the buggy. As the mill's whistle blew for work, the pointer barked a snappish bark, the St. Bernard took his place under the buggy.

"All ready, Cagy," said the Père.

"Gee up!" cried the stage-driver. "Good-by, everybody!" and on went the travelling show.

CHAPTER III.

A QUIET NOOK.

On the spacious lawn which surrounded a cosey house of the Queen Anne style and a neat wooden church, a gayly dressed child was playing, toward the close of a summer day. The lawn, with its close-shaven grass, dotted here and there with flowering shrubs, herbaceous plants, and flower-pots made of the trunks of pine and balsam, set with trailing vines, geraniums, and stock verbena, told that a lover of the beautiful in nature and art was the master. The house and church were surrounded by trees—the lordly pine that winter could not disrobe of his finery, the common but lovely maple, the deep-blushing mountain ash, with here and there the laughing lilacs vying with one another which should be most lavish of loveliness. Birds had found here their restful nook, and returned, each year, the swallow to the eaves, the robin to fill the maples with song, the yellow-bird to taunt with his wistful notes the caged canary, and many another warbler to blend his lay with the harmony of the woods. From the house a short run, and that by a well-kept path, the Salmon River sported along, now asleep, now wending its way by huge rocks, angry and ruffled, spitting yeasty foam, and in its discontent eating the soft sandy banks. If the observer was quiet, an otter might practically show his fishing propensities, a mink play hide-and-seek with its mate, a chipmunk erect his saucy tail and with charming grace nibble a beech-nut, held in his glossy paws. Now and then a deer, with pointed nose and antlers thrown back, would take his bath, eyes and ears in watch for sight or sound.

The child's companions were three dogs—a St. Bernard as body-servant, a huge mastiff, an indolent fellow, lying on the church-steps, and a pointer always in motion, the attacking party. His aim was to tumble the child by coming on a quick run and jumping on her with his paws, a trick that was rarely successful owing to the watchfulness of the St. Bernard, who met each jolly attack by a well-directed mouth-snap. The child taunted the vanquished, kissed, hugged close to her breast the burly victor, and coaxed to her ranks the lazy mastiff dozing in the shade.

A bell rang; the little maid became sedate, the pointer quiet, wisdom returned to the St. Bernard, the lazy mastiff with dignity arose. The bell was hung on the limb of a giant elm, and rung by a long cord. The bell-ringer was an aged man, strongly built and well preserved. Not a thread of gray was to be found in the well-combed heavy raven hair. His face was of an olive hue, lit up by large, coal-black eyes. His walk had a military air; his carriage was erect and graceful; his step as light as a child's. He rang the bell with bowed head, his lips curving in suppressed speech as if in prayer. With the last pull he put on his hat, shouted to the child, and whistled for the dogs. All came running and speaking to him.

The child was soon in his arms, kissing him, the dogs tugging at his trousers' legs.

"What do you ring that bell for, Napoleon?"

"Did you never hear a bell before, Genevieve, where you come from?"

"Yes; plenty of bells, but I never saw one on a tree."

"Well, child, the reason of that is because Père Monnier is too poor to put up a belfry; but we shouldn't look to the place where 'tis hung, but to the meaning. Folks don't do that nowadays. Many a good book has poor covers."

"But what is the bell for?" asked the child impatiently.

"What were the bells you saw for, Genevieve?"

"When a house was on fire. Then two big ponies and the engine came jumping down the street. The engine was full of bells, and men with funny hats; that's what the bells were for."

" Did you ever run after the engine ? "

" Before mamma was sick I used to run with the other girls; everybody runs. Good fun, Napoleon."

" Is that all you know of bells ? "

" I know one more, Napoleon—Chittery's bell on his push-cart. He used to come round every Monday, his old bell a-going it, calling rags. Mamma always said when he came to our door: 'Chittery, I am too poor even to have rags!' Then Chittery would tell mamma that poverty was a hard dog to shake, and give her a paper of pins or needles. I liked Chittery, for he always brought me gingerbread in his inside pocket. I don't like him as well as Charlie, for he gave me all his money, and was going to keep me, but he couldn't find work. Mamma couldn't find work. You find work all the time with Père Monnier. I guess he likes you. I like you. I like Père Monnier. I like Anna—everybody here. I am going to be good; then I won't be sent away—will I, Napoleon ? "

" Sent away! No indeed, Genevieve. You're a fixture like myself and Anna. When Père dies there will be a scattering, but, as he says, that's too long a time ahead to be worrying about. Père Monnier wouldn't part with a cat that he took a notion to, much less a Christian. You're a part and parcel of the whole concern. We all think you're just right; but what beats me, you little witch, is, you never heard what that bell means. That's the Angelus. Did you never hear that word where you come from?"

"Yes, I did. Mamma had that, but it was not the same. Hers was a picture; it came in a paper, and mamma just loved it. She pasted it over our bed. I remember it very well. I can shut my two eyes and see it just as plain as I see you. There was a boy and a girl with their heads just the way you hold yours when you ring the bell, and a wheelbarrow and a bag of something on it. It was a nice picture. Mamma said they were praying. It was a very nice picture—the nicest in the room."

"Ah, Genevieve, is that all you know about it?"

The child nodded her head.

"Then you don't know how to pray when it rings? I will teach you, and in a few evenings you will have it by heart, and you can steal up to the Père and say: 'I know the Angelus.' Then say it. That will tickle the Père. Don't tell him who taught you if he doesn't ask. The smarter you are the better you will please him. He won't be home for two weeks, and in that time you should have the full of my hat of all kinds of prayers ready for him."

"I'll have them if you teach me," said the child, kissing Napoleon. "I won't give you away."

"That's settled. There goes Anna's bell ding-dong! ding-dong! I'm your pony, so away we go, away we go, to eat puddings and pies, and everything good for a lady, a lady."

Tossing the child up and down in his arms he ran to the house, losing his ordinary gravity, followed by the dogs barking and caressing—their way of having a good time.

"Napoleon Brousseau, are you out of your head? Is it looney you're getting? Save your fits until the Père gets home. Put the child down or you'll jump her inside out. Are you not afraid that the dogs will jump up and scratch her? Between you and your dogs and your mad capers there will be no bringing up to that child. Says the Père when he brought her here: 'That's a present for Anna.' Not a word about Mr. Brousseau. Yet since the Père started for Montreal I have hardly crossed my eyes on the child. You'll tire her out, you and your saucy curs. When it's not hunting bees, it's hunting butterflies, and when there's none of them around, you have her side-saddled on one of your dogs. How do you know but one of them may turn up his nose some day and bite her, and supposin' she gets the 'phoby in her what then will become of you? I'll tell ye: you will have to get out of this country bag and baggage, and pretty lively too.

"You're laughing, Mr. Napoleon. I never saw one of your kind that was not able to do that. Faith, when the 'phoby comes, you'll guff on the wrong side of your mouth. I have seen folks a-laughing, folks just as spry as you, and crying before a year passed over their heads."

The speaker was a middle-aged woman, robust and sun-dyed, with a motherly face lit up by lustrous eyes, beaming goodness from morning to night.

The tale of "the little show-girl," as she called her, heard from the Père's lips in that wonderful way he had when appealing in behalf of charity, made Anna find the cosiest place in her heart for the little "motherless one."

If Anna had listened to the Père's recital in tears, so had Napoleon, a man of iron, one who knew not fear. A Corsican by birth, he came with many of his comrades to the States and fought through the Civil War, receiving at Antietam a leaden medal, as he called it, for bravery in the shape of the bullet he carried in his breast. A chance acquaintance in Libby Prison with William Cagy ripened into friendship which resulted in his visiting Squidville in the Adirondacks now and then. On one of these occasions he met Père Monnier, and was so taken with him that on his wife's death, which followed soon afterwards, he sold his little shop and came to live with him. The Père took the keenest delight in the old soldier, loved him with a brotherly affection, made him master of his dogs, horses, and all the cares of running the little establishment. He, on his part, was more frugal and economical than the soft-hearted Père, whose only knowledge of a pocket-book was its help in alleviating human misery.

The housekeeper and the old soldier loved the child and vied with each other in showing it.

"Well, dinner is on the table, and it's a good plan to eat it while it's hot," continued Anna, as she led the way to the neat dining-hall, which showed here, as in every part of the house, the artistic nature of Père Monnier. The walls were hung with pictures—bits of landscape that he had brought with him from Europe. Above the mantlepiece was a deer's head, a magnificent specimen of the Adirondacks, a trophy of the Père's prowess as a hunter.

The child's eyes, full of wonder, roamed from picture to picture, until they rested with keen delight on the deer's head. What kind of an animal was this? She had seen dogs, cats, and, on her weary tramp with Parenti, horses pulling heavy loads, lazy cows neck-deep in the brooks and pools, the shorn sheep, and the tiny, tottering lambs, with pitying call lessening their mother's pace. She had once slept all night in a tent with a group of gypsies, the men wiry and good-looking, the old women frightful; tawny, dirty children, and maidens tall, well-built, with snappy eyes, white teeth, and long coarse black hair bound in gold and silver clasps. They were good to her, and would have given Emil a mule in exchange for her, but he had promised Sal never to desert her until death. Emil had told her that these gypsies had all kinds of animals; and their queen, a wrinkled old dame, black as a Congo negress, had shown her a tame fox, a praying donkey, an educated pig, and green paroquets that knew the future and told it for the insignificant sum of ten cents. But all the animals she had seen were far from being as much to her taste as the one whose stuffed head held her attention. The big soft eyes, wells of pity, the graceful neck, the pointed, delicate nose, the funnel ears, the branching horns, the tight-fitting skin, all so gracefully formed,—all these chained and charmed the child.

"Child," said Anna, "you'll eat that deer's head up with your eyes. Sit down to your dinner; it's a-cooling. If you're around here long you'll hear and see enough of those things. They set my head crazy with their tales of hunting deer. The Père is no better than the rest of them. I don't see how folks put up with that Billy Buttons. He made me so mad the other day, waiting to finish his yarn, that I couldn't help saying: 'Bad luck to you, Billy Buttons!' And when I got home I found my kettle was boiled dry and the bottom of it burned out."

"Buttons served you right. I would like to see myself breaking up my story for any woman on the face of the earth," sneered Napoleon.

"You needn't bother your head about women, Mr. Napoleon; they give little thought to you. I pity them that was made for you and Buttons. I would like to see my man, instead of minding his business, spinning yarns to please others as lazy as himself," said Anna, pinning a napkin around the child's neck.

"You never had one—never will; so you're counting your chickens before they're hatched," said the ungallant Napoleon, helping the child to the steaming roast.

"Don't mind us, Genevieve," said Anna. "Napoleon, with his gab, would provoke a saint. Since a certain lady refused him he's death on all women. Keep right on eating, dear; don't let the deer's head bother you; you'll soon get enough of it, mark my words."

"But it's awful pretty," said the child. "I just love its eyes! I wish I had one."

"We'll get you a young one if you are a good girl," replied Napoleon. "That was the first deer Père Monnier ever shot."

"How did he kill him? Tell me, Napoleon.

Napoleon's eyes lit up, and a smile played on his face at the child's request. As Anna had predicted, there was no use to stop him; the tale was good, and any listener, even a child, was sufficient audience for the old soldier.

"Well, Genevieve, it was this way," and Napoleon

made a wave with his fork. "Père Monnier, when very young, had been a soldier. He is yet, but in a better army. He used to tell me and Buttons how handy he was with a gun in those old days. 'Now,' says Buttons one day, 'Père, if you want to get folks crazy about you, not that they don't love you well, you should become a bit of a deer-hunter. It would aid you a lot in your sermons, for if you knew all about the 'cuteness of the dogs and the cunning of the deer, you could introduce it and hit any one you liked. Say, how would this go in a sermon? John or Jim, mentioning no other names, but giving with it three or four tongue-jabs to fix your man, runs away from God like a deer from dogs; taking to the waters of sin, skulks in wickedness. That would be a dumbfounder. Another one, John or Jim, has a soul as black with sin as a burnt pine log. Supposin' you want to give them a bit on death, here's a whipper: Be prepared as a hunted deer, for you don't know the minute the dogs may be upon you. I told that to Cagy one time he was telling me about his folks being all hearty and long-livers. Besides, Père, it will give you plenty of raw air, the best meat your lungs can live on, and the walk will do you good. I warrant if we only get you there once, you'll find the way back.'

"I was longing myself for the whiz of a ball. Sometimes one becomes uncommonly lonely for old memories, so I urged the Père to accept Buttons' kind offer. Of course when Anna heard about it she reasoned the other way to show, as if we didn't know it, that she was a woman. The Père laughed, and would not say yes or no, so I hit upon a trick. I took out that pointer there and my gun and went shooting down in the woods. The shooting and the barking soon brought the Père to my side just as Macaveley treed a partridge.

" ' Give me a shot at her,' said the Père. ' I wonder if I can hit anything but the tree or the air, it's so long since I handled a trigger. I am loath to fire, for if I miss, you and Macaveley will feel I acted contemptibly.'

" ' Never mind,' says I, ' take the gun and pop her; the pot's ready, the water hot, and such a tasty bite is worth carrying home.' An old soldier never forgets that a ball was made for a target. It done my heart good to see his military cut coming back to him once the gun was in his hands. ' Take her in the head, Père,' says I, ' the body's the eating.'

" ' Give me a chance at any part of her,' said the Père.

" ' You know,' says I, ' how Anna hates to pluck a poorly killed chicken ? '

" ' Better try the gun, Napoleon.'

" ' No, Père; go on. You're sure to place a victim to your credit.'

"Well, 'Bang!' went the gun, and down came the bird with its head a clean cut. It was a beautiful piece of work.

"'Don't you think, Père, that you could bring down a deer after that?' says I.

"'I have courage now,' said the Père. 'You know I was rather afraid I had lost my aim, but the things of youth are hard to part with. Yes; I think I might go after the illustrations that Buttons suggests for my sermons.'"

"He's only beginning, dear," said Anna, "and so much work to be done this afternoon. Nothing troubles him."

Napoleon munched a bit of bread and then went on: "I saw Buttons and told him the story just as you have it—not a word less or more. My, but he was proud! 'Cagy must hear that,' said he, 'for he wants to go along as much as me, and he's capital in putting out dogs. He knows the woods like a book, that he does! The Père won't wait long before a deer tries his mettle. He'll find—but don't let on to him, for fear we scare him—that a treed partridge is easier to shoot than a running deer. He'll have to reckon with motion.'

"'Never mind that,' says I. 'Motion or no motion, it's my opinion that the deer's life is not worth a nickel once the Père levels his gun.'

"Early one morning the door-bell was jingling at

a great rate. I jumped from my bed, thinking that some one was preparing to take his departure and needed a word of advice from the Père. As soon as I turned the key in the door I knew by the barking that I was wrong. It was Buttons and Cagy with their rigs, ready for an early start. There had been a slight fluster of snow, so they wanted to have their hunt before it would go off.

"It's a habit of the Père with the first bell-pull to jump from his bed, as he says, 'Those who want me, want me quick,' though to tell the truth there be some who take him out without either rhyme or reason, just for the whim of it."

"Like old Goulet," broke in Anna, "who took him ten miles on a hurricane night, and when he got there the old villain was scolding his wife, and was full of the devil instead of sickness."

"Aye,—and what about the women?" continued Napoleon. "When their husbands scold them don't they go into fits? Don't they get him out? Don't they blame everything on the men? But, to take up the thread of my story, the Père was at my heels. 'Hitch up Molly,' says he, 'while I get my oils and pyx. Who's sick?'

"'Don't mind these things,' says I, laughing. 'It's only Buttons and Cagy and their rigs and dogs out for a hunt. They heard about your partridge-shooting, so they come to invite you to kill a tremendous buck that only waits the dogs to give you a sight of him. We won't have far to go either; that's the best of it. Cagy spied his track yesterday in Bill Lantry's sugar-bush.'

"'Well, Napoleon, get everything ready. I suppose we'd better go, seeing they came for us.'

"The Père went to dress, and I, an old campaigner, soon had the guns in shape, and the pack-basket filled with provisions. Hunting is hungry work. A bit of bread, a snack of meat, and a little wine are consoling when you have to sit on a stump for hours and not hear a whimper from the dogs, only the wearisome chatter of the bluejay flying from tree to tree as if he had a bee in his bonnet. Nobody who has once sat there without a bite will be again in the same predicament, and I don't blame him.

"Well, we were soon on the road, and in an hour's time by fast driving we had reached a lumber shanty and surprised three porcupines that had been there off and on for weeks, looking for salt and boring boards, as if they were augers. A few shots put them asleep. We chopped a half-burnt pine, and with the dry straw in the shanty soon had a fine blaze and a pan of Indian-meal porridge for the dogs. Dogs are like everything else. They want to break their fast before working. This talk about sending them out hungry is all moonshine. A game dog runs from pure cussedness. It's in him to go, and the stronger he is the livelier will his go be.

"Buttons was the captain, so he done the talking. 'Père and boys,' said he, 'Cagy will put out the dogs, and each man must stand on his runaway until I shoot my gun three times. That will be the signal to come in, that the hunt is off. We have not men enough to cover all the runaways, but I'm thinking that, if they run at all, they'll either go to the Hatch-brook or by the green timber. I will place you, Père and Napoleon, by the brook, while I take to the timber, and Cagy, after he's through, can join me. It won't take him long to start one of the big fellows.'

"So William Cagy tied two dogs to his belt and, lighting his pipe, off he went. Buttons shouldered his gun, and we, bidding him good luck and assuring him if his dogs would do us the honor of sending any of the big fellows our way they would receive a peppery reception, struck out for Hatch-brook, a quick half-mile run.

"The Père made him a cosey retreat behind a clump of willows, trimming them a bit the better to see. He drew from his pocket his breviary and began to read. I went a few rods further up, by the side of a deep hole, and, concealing myself, listened for the dogs. I was getting fidgety, when I heard their music, at first low and doubty, then strong and sure, coming as straight as a pin in my way. I danced, patted my gun as if she were a Christian, pulled up the trigger, levelled her, and impatiently waited for the deer. The dogs stopped; then down went my gun disgusted. Soon it commenced again, but it was making away from me this time, bearing a little in Buttons' direction. It went over the hill out of my hearing and I heard shots and shots, but none came from our party. 'That's just our luck,' says I. 'Some sneaks get the benefit of our dogs. We may as well give up.' I remembered Buttons' command to stick to our posts, so I sat there for hours imagining that the purr of the brook was a dog, then fooled trying to sleep, but only getting a doze, full of thoughts of my soldiering life. It was long after noon, between three and four, that I became so restless I could stand the wait no longer, so taking my gun I hurried over to see what the Père was doing with himself. I found him reading a little Latin book he called "Horace" which he used to carry in his hip-pocket and read whenever he went out fishing and sport was dull. Many a thing he translated out of that little book for me which made me think that common-sense is a pretty old article.

" 'Well, Napoleon, you must not let Buttons see you here. I'm told he's touchy if his commands are set aside,' said Père Monnier.

" 'Buttons cannot keep me shivering behind a

stump if his curs fool around the deer and chase them over the hill instead of bringing them here. I'm tired waiting and won't stand it any longer,' I said, a bit huffy.

"The Père laughed and bid me open the pack-basket and get out our lunch, which I did very quickly, being half famished. So we ate and chatted about old times—about Italy, where both of us had left a bit of our hearts. There's no land like it, and fortune is cruel to those whom it shows Italy and then banishes here.

"All was calm and quiet. Not a dog was to be seen or heard in any direction. The meal finished I lay down in very desperation to have a nod, to forget Buttons' orders and his silly dogs. The Père took out his book, saying: 'Napoleon, I must catch something to-day.' Hardly had he spoken when we heard the snappy cracking of the brush, and looking in the direction saw something cut through it like a knife. I pulled myself on my knees without making a sound. The Père was ready, the muzzle swaying like a clock's pendulum until it was time to strike the hour. On came the deer—that deer," pointing to the set-up head, "and into the stream he goes. I saw at a glance that the Père was unable to shoot—he was so paralyzed with his beauty. It was the finest scene I ever saw, far prettier than that," pointing to the etched Landseer. "There was the mountains wooded with the sheeny trees to the very top, the little brook lilting away like a Corsican maid putting her cat asleep in the sun, a silver snake cutting in two a bit of green plot. In the middle of the brook stood the deer at his leisure. He had been hunted and, hot from his long run, was glad to find something wet and cooling. Now and then he put his lips to the stream and spurted water over his steaming hide. Then he would stand still, point out his nose, throw up his ears, and, like the pointer there, incline his head this way and that way for sound.

"What a beauty he was then ! The big antlers polished like a flint-stone and branchy like a young tree, the great eyes dancing jigs and reels in his head, and the soft, nicely-curved sleek neck. Ah ! I won't forget that sight as long as I live. Every time I come into the dining-room off goes my mind in a twinkle to Hatch-brook. Of course a fellow like me that has been men-shooting in my day don't think much of putting even a good-looking deer to sleep, but then if I shot men it was because I done my duty. I had no bad feeling towards the poor lads my gun sent overboard. I must tell the truth, I did hate to shoot that deer."

"Well, if you shot men," interjected Anna, "in your day, you're changing, for I cannot get you to kill a chicken, you pretend to hate blood so much. I believe in my heart and soul, Napoleon Brousseau, that you just put it on to save you work. If you can boast of killing folk that done neither you nor yours hurt or harm, you can knock overboard chickens just as easy."

"Well, Anna, you're bound to bob up and down like the head of a loon." And Napoleon continued the tale of a deer.

"A dog's bark, hardly a sound to my ear, came from over the hill. The deer jumped.

"'Shoot, Père!' I cried. 'He'll be in the wood in a jiffy.'

"'Bang!' went the Père's Remington. It was followed by a splash. 'Buttons will see,' said I, 'that motion or no motion is all one to the Père.' When the smoke blew off there lay the deer dead as a hammer. I waded to my knees in the brook and tugged him to the Père.

"'Isn't he a beauty, Père?'

"'Well,' said the Père, 'he is a handsome fellow; about the finest-headed that runs in these woods. I was so taken with his beauty as he stood in the current that I could not muster courage to lower his stately head. The moment he jumped, the passion of sport, that prick of old nature so hard to subdue, spurred me, so here he lies, and yonder,' pointing to a hound swimming the stream, lapping its water in delight, 'is the dog that drove him to his ruin.'

"The dog came up to us, saw his prey, danced, shouted, rubbed his nose in our hands, kissed the Père's gun. 'Victory, Père,' says I, 'is something dear to man and dog. It flushes and makes everything feel good.'

"'For the time,' said the Père. 'But in man there is an afterthought which may change victory to sorrow.'

"'It's a blessing that dogs don't think,' I stammered out.

"Then came the noise of three shots, and Buttons and Cagy showed themselves on the opposite side of the brook a little downcast.

"'What luck?' asked Buttons.

"'Why didn't you drive in something?' said I, 'if it was only a water-rat?'

"'You must have been asleep,' said Cagy, his eyes jumping, his mouth making all kinds of curves. 'Mickey' (that was the dog's name) 'drove under your noses a monster. I had a sight of him; he was as big as an ox. Just think! he has been running nearly nine hours, and then he was far ahead of Mickey. Judge, Buttons, of the strength of that deer from these facts. It's too bad to let him go scot-free, but there's no use in crying over spilt milk.'

"'Which of you fired the shot,' asked Buttons, "for I heard a bang down the way? I guess you'll find, Père, that it is easier to shoot a frightened-to-death partridge, stuck in the corner of a tree, than a running deer. One waits for the bullet; the other runs away from it.'

"'Well,' said I, 'Buttons, if you had to live on the Père's leavings, you would soon be as lean as a rail. Come across and we'll show you that a deer is as easy to put asleep as a partridge. We give your deer a hot reception. Choke-cherries won't bother him any more.'

"Well, if you had seen their faces! They were beside themselves. In a jiffy they were with us.

"That settled the Père in their minds. Said Buttons to Cagy, 'He's the genuine stuff.' Said Cagy to Buttons, 'If that man can't make folks Christians, there's no use in trying.'"

Napoleon's tale was done.

"Is that all?" inquired the child, clambering on his knee and poking his nose with her little forefinger.

"It's more than we bargained for," said Anna, rising to fetch the mince pie. "Don't start him again. There's heaps of work to be done."

"Père Monnier is a great man, Napoleon. I am lonesome for him. I love him first, and then Anna and you just the same," said the child.

"Continue to love him first. It's the best way to please Anna and myself. It's neither sin nor blame to love the Père."

CHAPTER IV.

AN EVENING IDYLL.

"Come, Veeva," said Anna one evening, "let us take a stroll and pluck the nicest flowers we can get in the beds for the Père. He comes home to-night. Napoleon has gone to the train to meet him. He will soon be here, and I want you to learn to put fresh flowers on his desk every morning, just a tiny bouquet. He loves flowers, and if you do this little trick it will win his heart. Napoleon has been all over the world and knows everything worth knowing. He tells me the proper way to present bouquets is bound with a ribbon, and a card saying, '*My compliments;*' then your name. He says that's the way they do in Rome, and as the Holy Father lives there I'm sure that's the right way. But when you cannot handle the pen with any kind of a quiver, the mouth is the only thing that's left. If I could handle it like Napoleon I would never regret my loss of writing. But if everybody could do the same thing there would be no trade, and that wouldn't do, either. It's, after all, better the way it is. What one misses the others hit."

"Can't you write anything, Anna?"

"No, dear. As far as I went was to make my mark when I sold my farm. It was a cross I made, and I done it so neat that Mr. Dixon, who was the witness, said loud that the people could hear him all over: 'Anna, well done! That ties up things just as well as if you could imitate the curves of Professor Slithers.' And Mr. Dixon is a man that speaks his mind. He's like a well; you can see through his eyes to the bottom of his heart. I'm glad you're here, child, you can write for me. I have a lot of letters to be written, seeing it's nigh ten years since I had any written. It's just as well; I couldn't help my folks much, and what you don't know don't worry you much. I was getting a bit uneasy, when you came, about my brother John in Canada. It will take a lot of sheets to open my mind to him. I'll tire him with questions. So many things happen in a year, let alone ten, that it's a puzzle how we'll get the letter started. You might be thinking it up between now and the writing. I'm well—that will be after telling them that the weather is as fine as silk and as warm as an oven. Then you can ask them how they be, and if crops are good. Then we can keep at it, by fits and starts, until we finish it. There's no hurry. News is one commodity that's never stale."

"Will there be many big words in the letter?" asked the little maid, proud that she was to be the secretary of the artless old housekeeper.

"Small words, like little potatoes, if you have enough of them, will go in the end as far as big ones. I'm not particular, child. I warrant it's in you to spell near enough the meaning. What they cannot make out they have the privilege of guessing, and my brother John has changed if he don't come close to it. I knew him once to tell what a lassie was thinking about by reading her eyes. He saw what was what plainer than if it was in a book, for he's like myself, dumb in reading."

"I'll write all your letters, Anna; I like to write," said the child, throwing her arms around the housekeeper's neck as she bent to pluck a pansy. "Mamma used to make me write lots."

"She was a good mamma, bless her heart for it! But didn't you also go to school? I was never in the big cities, but Napoleon tells me there's schools in every street. Did you ever go to one of them?"

"No, Anna, I never went, because I had no good clothes, and mamma said the girls would make fun of me and call me 'Tatters.' One day I went to play with the scholars and they did just as mamma said and more, for they made faces and called me a ragpicker. I came home crying, and mamma said I ought to have taken her advice and kept to the playmates on my own street. That's what I got for not minding my mamma."

"Those city girls are awful bold. I see enough of them up here in summer," said Anna. "With their frills and flounces, yellow skins and peaked noses, it's telling them they have clothes to hide their ugliness. But clothes is not all, if you only knew it. They would give the world for your fresh face and bonny curls. Poverty is no disgrace. Sure the Lord Himself was poor. I heard the Père saying, one Sunday, that the foxes and the birds had more of a home than Him. And sure enough they had, one kind with their holes, the other with their nests. And I'll warrant these saucy lassies that made you cry were Christians. If these be the kind of them, may the Lord deliver us! Napoleon calls them hypocrites, and says there will be smash, some of these days, for the folk with the lying lips and bad hearts as be these rich city folk."

"Charlie said there would be 'smash,'" spoke the child, "and Sal wanted it. Mamma used to speak the same way. It will come, Anna—smash. Then their nice clothes and their schools—everything will be smash. I'll be glad."

"Faith, you're a knowing child—head and ears ahead of folks that be older," said the old housekeeper, eying her ward with laughing eyes, and running her hand through her curls up and down, much as she petted Jenny, the easy-living cat.

"And you, in a way, learned yourself, child? For of course your mother couldn't be around to help you," continued Anna. "Can you cipher, too?"

"What's that?" asked the laughing child, making a dash for a humming-bird that was hovering over a bunch of phlox, sipping its sweets and questioning its beauty by contrasts.

"Your mother surely taught you to make ones and twos and naughts, and count up to a hundred!" answered the housekeeper. "That's what we call ciphering. It's just as handy in its own place as book-reading, every bit. If you don't know it, you'll soon learn—mark my words! You have a skull on you for that."

"That's what you call ciphering? It's a funny word," said the child, "awfully funny! In the city we call it figuring. I can do that. Mamma taught me to add, subtract, and multiply. I can tell you how much twelve times twelve make. It is one hundred and forty-four."

"That beats anything I've heard in many a day," said the startled Anna, "coming out of a youngster's mouth. My, my! but you have a powerful count. Indeed, Genevieve, you may well think of your mother. But tell me, do you mind anything about your father? I'll warrant there's a stream of smartness on both sides of your house. Come here and tell me if you mind him. I never heard you speak about him."

The child sidled up to Anna and nestled her curls in the housekeeper's apron, her eyes upturned to those of the good old dame. It was a picture not to be forgotten,—age, mellow in kindness, supporting confiding childhood. Age was asking a question. Childhood prattled a satisfactory answer. The woman had never been accustomed to see deeper than the words which fell on her ear; she subjected them to no analysis. The child's ideas were no deeper than her speech.

They understood each other, and that is more than can be said of philosophers—that weary crew who find their occupation in misunderstanding one another.

"I'll tell you, Anna, what mamma said about papa. One day I was out playing and the boys and girls said, 'We have a papa and a mamma to fight for us, but Veeva has only a mamma, and she is of no account, she's always sick.' Then one of them pushed me, and I fell in the mud. Oh! I cried, Anna. I thought I would choke. I ran and told mamma, and she cried, too, so much that I said I would never tell her anything more, and I kept my word. Mamma had to lie down in bed, she was so weak; then she called me to her and kissed and kissed me, until my curls were all wet with her tears. She said: 'My darling, I want you to forget all about your papa; he was a bad man.' When she said this her eyes frightened me. 'If he had been good we would not be starving here to-day.'

"Then I said: 'Mamma, where is he?' 'I don't know, darling,' mamma said; 'he may be in the city, but wherever he is I don't want to see him. He took me away from a happy home, darling, and after you were born he went away, one day, after beating me, and I have not seen him since. I never will. I don't want to see him. O Genevieve, my darling, you must never, never, love anybody but your mamma!' Then she cried and cried, and I fell asleep.

"That's all she told me, Anna, of my wicked papa. If Charlie had been my papa he would not have gone and left us. I want never, never to see my bad papa. I only loved mamma, but now I'll love the Père, and you, and Napoleon. I'll always stay here. You will never send me away—will you, Anna?"

The old housekeeper had a human heart. It was beating loudly to the child's artless tale. The big, reeking tears galloping down the olive wrinkles told how the child had impressed her by tearing out a leaf from the book of her life.

"Now, Genevieve," said Anna in a half-choked tone, "don't call your father such hard names. He may have been unnatural—I'm thinking he was—but

God will deal with him for that. And, above all things, don't tell any one what you have told me. Your mamma didn't mean those words to go any further. She's dead and gone, may heaven be her bed! and, of course, she had to forget and forgive, so there's no use in loading your young years with old sores. It's better to forget him, or if you want to think of him, do it by praying that he'll have a chance to mend his ways. Your mamma has been like lots of women that married some sleek-faced, sugar-mouthed fellow, to find out later that the sleekness is varnish and that the sugar is salt. Dear, men are gay deceivers. For one good one you will see a dozen misfits. I cannot blame your mamma, dear, that she was caught. Hawks are always on the lookout for young birds that leave the nest too soon. I can't blame her. When foxes can be trapped, what's the use in talking? Nobody wants to be fooled if they can help it. I suppose she married the angel part; the devil came after. No, child, don't say a word about your folks, not a word, no matter who cross-questions you. Tell them to ask Père Monnier, and that will end the affair. I'll warrant you nobody will come gossiping around him. You have not been long in this house, but long enough to have a name. I'm told the Italian man that you were with called you one name, just as if you were a dog or a cat and hadn't been baptized like a human being. I am always afraid of these monkey-men. They don't seem to be just natural. Sure you must have remembered your other name. Every handle has something behind it. Wasn't your good mamma called Mrs. Something? When the neighbors came in didn't you hear them say, ' Good-day, Mrs. ——'?"

The child shook her head.

"Of course you did, dear. What was it? Just tell Anna."

"Mrs. Bain," said the child. "Sal when she came in would say: 'You're a bit easier to-day, Mrs. Bain.' Sal was good to mamma and me when she had something to divide, but work was hard to get, so she didn't have much. I didn't like Rob, though; he wouldn't let Sal give things away, if he knew it. Sal used to fool him by tying things for mamma in her skirts."

"Dear me!" said the housekeeper, "your memory's as fine as silk, and so long drawn out. I have no head upon me. You remember everything. Now your name is Genevieve Bain, and it's pretty, that's more than you can say of some names around these borders. Well, I cannot get that monkey-man out of my head; to throw away the best part of your name, and to whittle away the other part into something good enough for his monkey, but not for a Christian child."

"Oh! he was awful good to me, Anna," said the child. "I liked him. He bought me cakes, candies, and a ring—lots of things! He never whipped me. He said that he loved me more than Jocko."

"And he made such a speech as that, comparing a child to a monkey!" cried the indignant Anna.

The child continued: "He was very good to me, Anna. When I was tired, he took me on his back. I guess it was hard for him, he puffed away. I liked him—not as much as you and Charlie and Sal, but I liked him because he didn't whip me."

"A pity that he should kill the goose that was laying him his gold egg every day," rejoined Anna. "You were his living. But here I am chattering about dead folks! If he was kind to you, he has his reward long afore this. Poor man, he's dead, and I should let his bones rest. I suppose the most of us have enough to account for if we minded our own business. Now I think we have enough of flowers. When the Père comes you must run out and say: '*Bon soir, mon oncle,*' and clap your hands. That shows you are glad. Wait till you see the way Napoleon's brats of dogs will caper. These dogs know as much as a man. They'll bark, and jump, and wag their tails, and carry on as if they were crazy. I believe Napoleon puts them up to it in order that the Père should like them. What he likes there's no use making complaints against. So that's the way Napoleon keeps his useless dog-show, eating more than we do. These dogs might tear down the house and Napoleon would say they were playing. One of them stole my roast, and says Mr. Napoleon, 'Anna, don't you know it's the nature of the animal to eat meat when it comes handy?' Well, I want you to be as sharp as Napoleon's dogs. I want you to caper a bit and say what I told you. You will remember it. Just try and say it over, '*Bon soir, mon oncle,*' which means 'Good-evening, uncle.'"

The child repeated the phrase in a way that pleased Anna, who continued:

"Why, Genevieve, as sure as you are there, it will be no time before you learn French. Napoleon will have you on his knee learning you to sing his songs. He tells me that his best songs are in Italian, but I cannot tell what they're about, and he wouldn't give me that much satisfaction as to translate them. I have my own opinion that I don't miss much. I never liked the monkey-men's gibberish, anyway. Did the Italian man sing any for you when you were trudging with his show?"

"Oh, he sang often," replied the child, "about his '*bella Italia.*' That's 'pretty Italy,' Anna. He said he used to be happy out there, and then he would sit down and sing and cry and get up and say, 'What's the use? It's all over now. I'll never see my home again.' He said he had donkeys, goats, and wine, and lots of nice things where he came from, and that there was nothing nice in this country. In *bella Italia*, he said, there were flowers, and nice birds singing night and day, and music and dancing, but here there was nothing but work; no birds but dirty little sparrows, chattering like padrones when you don't do enough work; the music was all sound and Dutchy, and the dancing silly stuff. In his country if you were sick friends would share; but here everybody is for themselves. That's what he said, and then he would always finish by saying, 'What's the use? We must go through it. Get up; we'll have to go and earn a meal.''

"The poor man!" said Anna. "He had his own load to carry, but if he had been spared to stroll the country a bit he could have seen things to the contrary. I'm sure there's more birds than chattering sparrows. He would be a saucy bird in his country that would fill his mouth and pipe it off with the robin when he is at his best. As for flowers, they are to be had for the gathering. Then I wish he had seen our dances; they would have done him good. Oh, my, Genevieve! I'm out of that work now, but the sound of Nick Poulet's fiddle makes me stamp like a horse when you give him oats. I suppose it's in me. When I was young I did like the floor, no doubt of that. I was always bespoken for every dance. I would have to refuse a dozen times and more in one evening. But here I am clattering about myself to a slip of a child when I should be preparing the Père's supper. Come, Genevieve, and bring your bouquet. I will show you how to place it."

The train was late; nothing unusual in that part of the country. The people were patient. Grumbling is a city art. Mountain people have too many tales to tell, too many jokes to crack, to let a few minutes' or even a few hours' disappointment in the time of a train schedule annoy them.

The station, or, to use its full name, " Owlville Depot," a name painted right across the station's forehead in awkward letters, was large enough to hold a desk for the youthful but dignified clerk.

It was a great convenience to have the train stop here, and little inconveniences were nothing to the mountaineers. In winter the depot was large enough, and in summer who would care to leave the glorious landscape view of the mountains and the winding river for this human hen-coop?—to use a tart phrase of William Buttons, Squidville's postmaster, and as apt a phrase-maker as is known in these parts. The artistic taste of the clerk was easily seen. The walls of this "human coop" were pasted with photographs of artists, cigarette prizes (the clerk being a great admirer of my Lady Nicotine in that dress), newspaper prints of prize-fighters, and, high above them, a large picture of a saddled donkey looking for a rider.

Napoleon, who had travelled much and studied man under many skies, cared little for the clerk's dignity. By intuition the youthful official seemed to know this and take the old soldier's bluffness with laugh and banter, a manner which changed with the coming of a native into the discourse. Napoleon had the audacity, for that was the name given to it by several young ladies who admired the clerk's gray eyes, the parting of his hair, the cut of his shoes and their daily fine polish, to sit at the clerk's desk, light a cigar, and puff away, not even leaving the favored seat at the official's presence. To one of the young ladies who was not content with disdain pictured on her face, but who had to bring, as Napoleon later termed it, "her mouth machinery into play," the old soldier, common-sense like, said: "Better for you to be at home washing dishes than here falling in love with airs. It's not the boy you're after; it's his hair-cut and shoe-polish. See how the donkey winks at you."

That was enough to vanquish the group of maidens. It brought disaster on their cause, for the quick-witted urchins dubbed the waiting maidens "hair-cut," "shoe-polish," and divers other names suggested by Napoleon's invective. These names, flung with vehemence from behind freight-cars, were the means of keeping the ladies at home, much to the clerk's disgust. He should not be blamed. He was young and good-looking, and woman's flattery is the dearest gift of the gods.

There was a sharp, prolonged whistle. The clerk arose, and graciously nodding to Napoleon, remarked:

"Mr. Brousseau, your train. I hope the Père will not disappoint you."

The depot was speedily deserted for the platform, and anxious eyes were strained in the direction of the whistle.

A puff of dark, gray smoke and the Montreal train had rounded the curve and was drawing into the little mountain station to puff and pant for a few moments, and then to speed over the hills.

Of late years Owlville had assumed importance enough to be noted in a guide-book as the stopping-place for Colonel Phipps' mammoth mountain resort. The waiting stage and the prancing horses were to carry the coming passengers through a stretch of six miles of charmingly kept road to the Colonel's far-famed inn.

"All for Phipps' this way," shouted a burly driver.

A few men and a crowd of ladies, young and old, carrying alpenstocks and little bundles wrapped in shawls held with hand-straps, hurried after.

One of the last to leave the train was a tall, athletic

man in priestly garb, a large bundle in his hand, evidently books. His pockets bulged with magazines and papers, showing their ends over the pockets' flaps.

His face was finely chiselled, one of those faces that would please a Grecian sculptor in the best age of Greece. It was a face of wondrous beauty and intelligence, crowned with long raven-black hair carelessly brushed back.

A stately St. Bernard wagged his tail, a sign for a savage-looking mastiff to open his huge red jaws, showing depth of mouth which made the ladies in Col. Phipps' stage huddle together at his barking. How glorious to the long-absent master is the loud rolling welcome of his dog! A pointer, ill-behaved, jumped to and fro, caught his tail and pirouetted like a ballet-dancer.

"I'm awful afraid of those savage dogs," said a sallow spinster to the stage-man. "Get us out of here as quick as you can. It's an outrage to allow any man to have such dogs. Wasn't it lucky that I left my poodle at home? Dear me, poor Dandy! How these brutes would have torn you to pieces! This is monstrous. I must see the Colonel. These dogs should be shot. I have no doubt they will be shot."

"Shoot *them* dogs!" said the driver huskily. "I would like to see any man shoot them and me around. I would make him drink the same medicine."

"Men and dogs up here," retorted the spinster low enough to escape the stage-man's ears, "are all savages. What a brutish fellow that driver is! Has a mouth on him like the mastiff. Barking fits it better than speaking. I wonder what the Colonel is thinking about to have such a villainous man in his employ. The Colonel shall hear before I sleep every word of his rudeness."

"Gee up, there, Frank! Straighten out, Nelly, and don't be a-worrying your partner! Everybody be comfortable," yelled the driver, and off went Colonel Phipps' stage.

"The stage is pretty full to-night, Napoleon," said the man in the priestly garb, jumping into the buggy.

"Yes, Père; Poulet has a load. How did you fare since you left us? You're looking well. What have you got in those bundles? Books, I warrant! Lord, Père, it's a wonder to me that your skull doesn't give up with reading! It's telling ye that learning don't take up much room. If it did, what would become of you? When Anna sees these books she'll have a fit. I was so full of gab on seeing you that I forgot to tell you of the child."

"That's the first question I wanted to ask you," said the Père, laughing, "but you gave me no chance. Was she lonesome? See what it is, Napoleon, to have a youngster in the house. I am glad to come home. I was lonesome for our little girl. One of my friends said to me: 'Why, Père Monnier, you are uneasy. I never saw you in that state before.'

"Yes; I was uneasy. I thought that Anna might not understand the child, a hundred foolish things came to my mind. I am afraid our girl will steal some of my book-time, but it's just as well. She is a charming child, so bright! I long to see her. Did you notice how jauntily she tosses her curls? She brings to my mind memories of the only sister I had, who left us at her age. We will have her chattering French in no time; then she'll have the key to Anna's heart."

"Bless your soul, Père, she has the key already. Anna thinks there's nothing like her on two feet. The other night she fell asleep on Anna's lap, her little arms around Anna's neck. Says I, just for a joke: 'Let me take the baby.' Well, if you had seen the eyes that Anna gave me! 'I'm sure,' says she, 'the child's in as good hands as if she was in yours, and maybe better.'"

"I am so glad the child has found a home," said the Père. "Poor child! like so many left friendless, tossed about by every wind. She will grow up a fine young lady, Napoleon, and be our great consolation in days to come. God sent her to us, and we will take good care of His gift."

"Well, Père, don't put too much learning in her

head; it doesn't work well with girls. As Anna says, it has set out of kilter many a one's head. There's no denying that. Besides it fills them with airs. But what am I talking about, as if you didn't know your own business, and wanted the likes of me to be catechizing you! She's smart. What learning you give her she'll swallow like a fish; that's my opinion. The few prayers and words in French I told her she picked up in a jiffy. She'll astonish you with what she has picked up since you went away. You have only to tell her a thing once; after that you have no bother. It's lying there ready for use. When she puts anything away it's she that knows how to find it. Her memory is as fresh as a daisy. She's useful to me as a kind of a memorandum, locating where I drop shovels, rakes, and other things with the best intention of finding them. Open confessions, I often heard you say, Père, were good for the soul. So I'm telling you one of my failings and giving thanks that I have found a cure."

There was a hearty laugh from both men, tickling the dogs to romp and riot in front of the easy-going, well-mannered pony.

Their noise brought the child to the parsonage door.

Père Monnier, as he jumped from his buggy, caught a glimpse of the slight figure that so impatiently awaited his coming.

"Uncle," she cried, "come to Genevieve."

An Evening Idyll.

"Run to me, my pet," shouted the Père, holding out his arms and bending down. The child was soon in his arms, a bouquet in her hands, a kiss on her lips to welcome the stranger home.

Anna ran to the door " to get a bit of a look of how the Père stood it."

When she saw him carrying Genevieve, who was pinning a bunch of flowers on his coat-lapel, tears of joy ran down her cheeks, hastily scattered over her face by what she called her apron-wipe. As she turned on her heel to hurry up her supper her eye caught Napoleon carrying a huge bundle. Sorrow struck her heart.

"More books, books, books! Now he'll be up late and early poking into them, and pulling out of them, until he runs to a shadow. If he dies what use will be his learning? But I shouldn't be talkin' the way I do. I suppose learnin' is as useful up above as down here; but how will he make out for want of books? I often think about that."

The smell of savory steak and onions banished such deep cogitations, so she ran to her pan and became absorbed in ordinary things.

"You were lonesome while I was away, Genevieve! I thought Napoleon, with all his stories about dogs, deer, and wars, would have completely won your heart. Then Anna, with her pies and cookies, I thought would——"

Genevieve prevented him from finishing the sentence by putting her open little hand on the Père's mouth, and whispering in his ear, with that coy look in the eyes that only childhood has : " I like Napoleon and Anna, but they are not my uncle."

" ' I see,' said the blind man, even if your grammar needs a patch." And Père Monnier, to use the expressive words of Napoleon, marched to the house as proud as a peacock when the sun is dancing on his tail.

On his desk was a huge bouquet, lilies, asters, marigolds, pansies, and violets, artistically blended, and gracefully tied with a blue string from whence hung a note written in a childish hand.

" Let me down. I must run to Anna and help her to set the table. You want to read your letters and papers. I put them on your desk in two piles. I sharpened your blue pencil, and found your paperknife, and dusted all your books. I can fix your room just as good as Anna, and I don't hate books. I like them. The man who gave me a dollar—Charlie, a nice man—he had lots of books. All nice men have books. You have more books than Charlie. Let me down. I can get flowers for the table before you get through your mail."

" Jump down, then, my golden lass. I would not part with you for the world. I have brought for you from Montreal a reader, a speller, an arithmetic, and when we finish those we will have more, until you can feel just at home in this old tattered library of mine. It will not be many years, if God spares you to me, before you will be able to read that old book you see always lying open on my desk, Count Henry's Dante. It has a tale good to be told some summer evening under the maples, when flowers are all abloom and birds are singing. Go to Anna, dear."

"Golden lass, golden lass!" muttered the retreating child. "That's what Charlie called me. All good people call me that. I wonder if I shall ever meet Charlie. He lives in the big city, so far away. I walked and walked so much to come here. The big city must be far, far away. I wonder if uncle was ever so far. He might take me there, some day, and Sal would show him where the big men put my mamma."

"Well, well! what a notion that child has—to pluck such a pretty bouquet for my desk! I must see what she has written. These little things show fine blood. From them Charles Lamb would have argued nobility. She delights in capitals, probably thinking they give dignity and tone.

> "*To My Uncle*
> *With my Heart*
> *From his little Girl*
>   GENEVIEVE B.
>   MONNIER*"

"The child could not give more, and what a fancy to adopt my name! She wishes not only to be of my household, but of my kin. I wonder what B. stands for. Some childish fancy, I presume. I will not ask her. She is surely, little lassie, donating enough. How lucky I was to come by way of Dixon's pulp-mill! Many a time I have thought what obligations parents owe to God in sending them children. Yet how many shirk them and pay no attention to their bringing up! It will be different in Genevieve's case. I have an odd theory long held that children may be moulded into any form. I have now a chance to put my theory into practice and make of Genevieve a noble Christian woman. It is true I know nothing of her people. Her heredity is to me a closed book. As to her early environment, it could not be much worse. After living in the slums of New York and tramping the country with an ignorant showman she could hardly be expected to be refined. Genevieve shall be made to forget the past, and amid our surroundings shall blossom into fairness and loveliness. Education can do anything."

The Père sat down in his easy-chair, mechanically opening his letters and papers, paying little or no attention to their contents. He was indulging in a dream. Genevieve was to grow up thoroughly educated, his pupil, a joy to his old age. Death alone was to separate them. She was to do errands of mercy, to teach catechism, feed his doves and hens, train his dogs, decorate the little church, read to him, write for him, to do, ran his dream, the thousand little things which sweeten life. On his part duty would be done. He would begin to teach and mould the little treasure that the good Master had sent to his household. In the morning Genevieve should go to school, and what the school lacked would be made up by the home-training. Anna could teach an unswerving patience under all difficulties. Patience, obedience, charity, and piety were virtues that dwelt in his humble cottage, and these were to chisel the golden lass into fair womanhood.

So ran the dreams of Père Monnier, and they might have continued, for dream-stuff is easy to spin, had not Genevieve and the mastiff romped into his study, the barking of the dog as well as the child's gladsome voice telling him that "Anna was ready and supper was set." Just then the Angelus bell sent its message of peace over valley and highland. The Père rose and bowed, answering the bell in Latin, as Napoleon said, with his rich sonorous voice; the child imitated and tried to catch his words; the dog lay down to watch his master's face; Anna prayed for everybody; Napoleon, pulling reverently the bell-rope, remembered his fallen comrades, and lived over his battles.

The sound of the bell died tenderly away amongst the flowers. Père Monnier said laughingly:

"Praying is good for the appetite, Genevieve."

Napoleon, whistling, opened the door. The dogs joined him in the chorus. Anna made a remark about "the ease some folks turn from praying to whistling."

Supper was hot and steaming. To the usual grace Père Monnier added a silent prayer for Genevieve.

CHAPTER V.

A COUNTRY SCHOOL.

"WELL, what a charming princess they have made out of Genevieve! What a dress! As white as snow, and as smooth as a planed board! It's silk, I'm thinking. And red shoes, and shining things in your hair. You're the nearest thing I ever saw to the angels my mother used to tell me about. You're only wanting in one thing—that's wings, and there is no telling when you will get a pair of them and fly away. I'm giving you warning, if you do, that I'll surely shoot; and mind you, my little laughing girl, when I shoot, off goes the gun and something is bound to tumble. Many a thing I have seen run away from me in a hurry, I suppose laughing at just how it fooled me, but I changed its tune in double-quick time, and made it go easy and have better manners."

Napoleon laughed loudly at his brag.

"So you would shoot me? That is all you care about angels, Napoleon."

"Don't intoggerate me too much, and if you do, be sure you quote me just as I am. I wouldn't shoot you. How could I do that? It's only your wings—

to keep you at home with us. Didn't I say there was no telling when you will get a pair of wings? And do you think I would let you use them to leave us? It's all fooling, anyway. Come to my arms until I feel your weight."

"Well," said Père Monnier, stepping out from his own doorstep, "you're in a good place, Genevieve, but I fear Napoleon will muss your clothes. If he does, Anna's wrath, like a whirlwind, will surround him. You know your dress is Anna's masterpiece in ironing."

"Where are you bound for?" asked Napoleon, swinging Genevieve in his arms, and heeding little the threat of Anna.

"Where you, Napoleon, spent little of your time, and, if the sayings of somebody's tongue be repeated, that time was ungraciously given. If your head was as old then as it is now—but what use to annoy you. Genevieve and I are going to school. The new term begins to-day, so I am going to introduce her. After to-day you will see that she gets there in time."

"Annoy me! I would be easily annoyed," muttered Napoleon as he went leisurely about his work, throwing his eyes now and then on the tall, athletic frame of his scholarly master leading the lithe figure by the hand to her first school task. He could not help saying to himself: "All of that man's life is spent for other folks; not a drop to him more than me. It's well he don't look for his pay down here. Many's the one he has done for, and little thanks followed the doing. But I trust the youngster is of different stuff; at least she looks it."

Anna was peeping out of the window with similar feelings. The hours she had spent on the child's dress were more than repaid, for she knew that priest and child were walking along, hand in hand, proud of each other. She went back to her work.

Père Monnier and Genevieve clambered up the hill on which was perched the No. 9 schoolhouse under the management of Miss Ruth Croydon. The schoolhouse was of the common district-school class built of wood, carelessly thrown together.

In the country as well as in the town there is an idea that public money comes easily and should go in the same way. The mason and carpenter holding these ideas did their work quickly and charged as much as they could get. Under such conditions No. 9 had more resemblance to a painted barn than to a home of learning. The interior gave the builders as little thought as the exterior. It had been hastily boarded with rough "cull" lumber, opening into wide cracks in all directions.

The artistic taste of the mistress and her pupils was seen in their attempts to shut the cracks and crannies from view by chromos of fruit and flowers and lithographs mostly representing some sentimental scene in love's young dream. One over the rough table, which was dignified by the name of the teacher's desk, was unusually conspicuous, and was emphasized as important by a framework of fringed ribbon. It represented a maiden, sad and languid, gazing on the back of a rather pudgy man who was evidently going from the languid maid at a slow pace, yet, from a study of the maid's face, at a pace that kills.

Under the picture was written, "The Die is Cast," leaving the onlooker who is blessed with imagination to weave many a story. Some of the children, to escape from school drudgery, lay back on their seats, and in their quickly spun tales identified Miss Ruth Croydon with the picture girl, and the man as one of the many to whom she had presented a mitten—a mountain method of killing masculine love at the first shot. When on a memorable occasion a bright-eyed little dreamer showed her mind-spinning to a playmate who loved favor more than friendship, and the little spinner was brought before the Croydon correction-box, their teacher won all hearts, especially those of the larger girls, by discharging the prisoner with the remark that pictures were truly symbolic of human life, and that that picture represented a phase in every girlish life.

"A man may love a girl," she continued, "and the girl may love him, and he may ask her, and she has to say *No* to that breaking heart because—well, simply because the home needs her a little longer, and that opportunity, thrown away, may be her last."

There were tears in her eyes, and in those of the little prisoner whose mind was sorrow-bruised at its spinning.

The desks were of plain deal boards whittled with knives and splashed with ink, the happy secret work of many a boyish and girlish offender. Some maps, yellow with smoke and tattered with the fingers of youth, a few charts prematurely old and fantastically ornamented with drawings of monkeys, kangaroos, and other animals, the work of boyish fancy, hung on the walls. The blackboard had lost a leg, a loss that made it creak at every incoming and outgoing scholar. There was little hope that a leg might come. The trustees, elected by popular franchise, were ignorant men who sailed under the flag of cutting down expenses and making the taxes less, a flag dear to the farmers' hearts. A few educated reading men had at various times pleaded for better schools, more comfort for the children, but their arguments were soon overborne by the ignorant crying out against increased taxes, and repeating the time-worn argument that what was good enough when they went to school was good enough for their children. This argument gained the votes, and the votes made trustees.

The trustees held that all was well, and that

what was well should under no consideration be touched.

They owned to another duty, and that was following the wish of their electors " to scour the country for cheap teachers." "Any miss with a school certifier who could read, write, and count was good enough to teach the youngsters all they wanted."

As the "certifiers" came from commissioners put there by the people who made the trustees, and owing to that spirit of fraternity in politics, any girl favored by the trustee was sure of the document. Examinations might be, to use their phrase, "cooked for any mouth."

Under such a *régime* the district schools were mostly under the care of silly young girls without fitness, who made a few dollars weekly by letting the children take care of themselves, while they entertained their several suitors. The No. 9 school was an exception in regard to its teacher. Ruth Croydon had to teach on the same terms as the others, but her fitness and training were unquestionable; and her conscience would not allow her to do less than she was able for the lowliest child.

Circumstances had penned her life in a mountain village, and poverty had necessarily been her companion.

Yet she was uncomplaining; to the majority she appeared to be satisfied; to the trustees, perfectly contented. She had visions of a fairer past, and hope spoke of a happier future. With these softening the suffering present she turned a smiling face to the world, knowing that it would take the surface for the depths.

Economy comes by practice, and Ruth Croydon learned to live on the pittance gingerly doled out by the trustees of No. 9. Small as it was, it was sufficient to keep her old blind father in ease and decency. From the wreck of his fortune he had luckily been able to save a pleasant cottage and a few acres of good soil.

Thus rent was saved, and by the exertion of Miss Ruth the few acres, well watched and cultivated, gave, as her father boasted, "a vegetable and potato sufficiency for any two in the land."

Ruth's spring and summer evenings were passed in the garden hoeing and weeding, to get, as she laughingly put it, "a little nourishing exercise after the stifling atmosphere of her school."

Some women-folk at Mag Purdy's quilting-bee had passed a whole evening discussing this excuse. Their conclusion was that Ruth, born gentle and well-off, dropping down a peg, wanted to cover up the right reason which Mag Purdy forcibly declared to be "not being able to hire a man."

"Why in thunder," said one of the quilters, making her nose and upper lip meet, "don't she marry like any other girl, and have a man of her own to work the garden? Then she could work her airs better and stay in the house. This business of swelling it on nothing don't do amid plain-living folk as we be. It may go in the city where the folks, I'm told, don't want to be themselves."

There was a sneering laugh, making the speaker look a shade more stupid. The shade gradually passed with the speech of Mag Purdy.

"Well, Mrs. Brie, you're talking like a three-year-old young one. Ruth Croydon marry a man! Show me the man that's good enough for her. What man in these parts could give her all the didos she would be expectin'? To begin with, she's a musicker, and what kind of a musicker be she? Do you think, if you went to her house from now until next year, that she would condescend to play a hymn or a small tune? When young Ike, my brother's son, as you all know, a boy as full of music as a big sea-shell, and as lively as a chipmunk, asked her to organ out for him, he whistling it for her to catch as sweet a tune as ever you or me heard, conscience! I'm not lying, if she didn't tell him right to his face: 'Ike, I can't copy your sweet mouth with my pianny.' You may just think how he felt! 'Aunt,' says he, 'I thought I was blind till I come at myself.' I asked her—now I'm not at the hearsay—to play me one of Watts' hymns, and to steer her I lilted it. Then I gave her a verse:

"'Shepherds, rejoice, lift up your eyes,
And send your fears away:
News from the region of the skies:
Salvation's born to-day.'

Well, she just looked at me as if I was something from away off that she couldn't just place. 'Watts,' says she—mind her impudence!—'I regret, Miss Purdy, is not on my list, and I don't feel like putting him there when there is so much better—the classics.' She a kind of puzzled me, and as I am the last woman to make a break, 'Who be these classics?' says I, 'that count themselves better than Watts? Curious thing I never heard of them, and I've heard and sung pretty much all that's going.' Well, she went on explainin' until I was deaf, and when she was done I knew as much as ever. There's no gainsaying it (the divil his due every time), she's clever with the tongue. Then look at the books she has filled with all kinds of schooling. I was told by the Jew peddler that he met her on the road, and says he, wanting to be friendly in his own queer way, 'Wee gaits,' which I believe is 'Good-morning to you, Miss.' She could have answered him all day in his own gibber. He thinks she fell from the clouds and is waitin' for a stiff breeze to carry her back. He had a letter from home a twelvemonth before, but he couldn't read it, so he carried it in his jacket, takin' it out now and then to kiss it and cry over it like a child. So when she gibbered, out of his jacket he whipped it, and, conscience! she read it in a minute. You ought to hear him tell it! Now she writes and reads his letters. What would one of our one-tongued boys do with such a woman?"

"I heard one of the boys did go after her with intentions on her, that was a near relation of my own, who's a school-teacher now, but she treated him as you would a baby, letting him toddle around, giving him an eye now and then."

"It would take a book-writer or a minister to cope with that girl. She's plainly out of her element in these parts. Her place is in a picture-book. It's too bad to be born before your time, and a pity that there ain't in the world nice places to suit us all. I'm content—plain Mag, no airs, no gibberish, and any one burning me for a softy would find wisdom in the ashes."

"I think you're too sore on her, too sore entirely," said a kind woman (there is always one in a crowd). "I'm not takin' up with her faults. She's human like the rest of us, and, as Deacon Spratt says, 'who's not, let them be up and pelting stones.' My man, I think, would die for her. When our children had the fever and friends made themselves as scarce as white crows, Miss Ruth came every day, tramping through the snows, and give my children their medicine, and fussed with them as if they were her own, and I don't mind sayin', but she brought them bits of appetitin' things to cool their systems, which were like boilin' ovens. Now we was nothin' to her to do that. I reckon that's what you call charity, and says Minister Gliggins, one day he met her in my house putting the baby to sleep: 'Bess,' says he, 'it's Paul himself that says that kind of charity,' pointin' to Miss Ruth, 'covereth a multitude of sins,' and I'm of the same mind. Talk is easy; it costs nothin', but to come and set in my house during the fever—well, I'll make no bones about it: there was just one in the parish able to do it, and she be Ruth Croydon.

"Mr. Gliggins always said her music was high, and, so long as it's not a-going in the church, it's her business, if I don't mistake. About marryin', let everybody look to home. If you don't meet the right mate, you'll soon find to your cost that there is worse things in life than being an old maid. Ruth Croydon has been amongst us for a few years, and I call her a lady of the first water."

The conversation was quickly turned to the weather and crops, a subject which never tires in the country. It is in some way a fascinating topic, bringing into speech those who are most barren of ideas.

"And this is your school, child," said Père Monnier, as he halted in front of No. 9. "I know you will be a good little girl, and study hard and get some prizes. Just think how Anna and Napoleon will feel when you bring home your first prize. They will be perfectly crazy with joy, even the dogs will turn out to greet you, and I'll have a new dress for Miss Somebody. You will like your teacher very much, for she is a fine, intelligent young lady. Don't you hear the children reciting? Just listen—c-a-t! That spells *cat*. What fun they have! I wish I was a little boy again. O Genevieve, you don't know what it is to be young! You will, child; but then youth will have fled."

"I know who 'Miss Somebody' is, uncle, and she is going to have the dress; but she won't bring the prize to Anna or Napoleon, but to——" Genevieve was looking in his face, her eyes talking merrily to his heart.

"I know to whom," said Père Monnier.

The child nodded assent.

Ruth Croydon, being told by a scholar who paid more attention to the door and the open fields beyond than to his books that Père Monnier was coming to inspect something, gave the school a recess for a few minutes and came towards the door.

How the children scampered past her hatless, pell-mell, pushing and tapping one another, secretly praying that Père Monnier would come inspecting every day!

"I have brought you a pupil, Miss Croydon," said the priest, extending his hand. "She is small, but, as we say in the mountains, good goods are put up in small packages."

"May I ask the name?" said Miss Croydon.

Before Père Monnier had time to speak the child answered:

"My name is Genevieve Bain Monnier."

"Ah!" said Miss Croydon with a smile, "you ought to be smart! I shall do everything I can for your niece. It will be her fault if she does not succeed."

"I know that you have, really, Miss Croydon, done wonders with the children. Boys and girls who have been branded as dunces, and beaten and kept in after school day after day, have become bright and studious. I don't see how you do it. Napoleon thinks you have some kind of glamour that you throw over them."

"Napoleon, Père Monnier, is not wrong. I cast around them kindness. Correct me if I am wrong, but I think it was one of your sweetest saints who uttered a wonderful truth when he said: 'We can catch more flies with honey than with vinegar.' I never met, and never will meet, a child that I could not lasso with kindness. Bad boys and bad girls are made so by selfishness. Whips are the instruments of tyrants. Torture never made a man love his fellow-man. They say that whipping increases love in dogs. It is one of those old sayings which mean nothing. I know better. But if it were so, dogs and men are different."

"You will find it easy to lasso Genevieve," replied Père Monnier. "I think your speech has won her heart. I am of your mind in holding the doctrine of the good saint, and I think Napoleon would sustain your ideas on the dog question. I have heard him tell some wonderful stories of dogs remembering for years and years those who gave them blows.

"I believe also that kindness can do anything with youth. This talk of heredity and environment is absurd. Youth is like the potter's clay: you can mould it into any shape you will by kindness. I am sure you can kill any heredity-germs; but that theory is nonsense. A new environment will make the old forgotten."

He was looking at Genevieve, dreaming how he should mould her into an ideal Christian woman.

Then the children, hearing that a new pupil was coming to their school, shyly and inquisitively drew around Genevieve, one bold little tot touching her dress.

"Girls," said the teacher, "this is Genevieve Monnier, your little friend. On her account I shall give you ten minutes more of recess. You will be kind and take her along, show her the playground and make her feel at home. Genevieve, you can go."

There was a long cheer, and Genevieve was regularly adopted into the comradeship of No. 9. She was soon running and shouting, calling her playmates by name as if they were old-time friends. How easy to make friendships in youth—beautiful youth, when kindness is king and love is showered on all !

Père Monnier, well pleased, was about to return when Miss Croydon pleasantly remarked that she had long determined to call at Père Monnier's on a begging expedition.

"Now," she continued, "seeing you are here I might as well unbosom myself. My little stock of books is pretty well exhausted, that is—I fear I will have to be roundabout in my speech—exhausted as far as my father is concerned. I should have said that my stock was not large, yet enough for all my wants. I have Chaucer, Spenser, Wordsworth, Charles Lamb, Hazlitt, and Leigh Hunt, and a dear but tattered edition of Scott. I am not badly off. In fact I could live on them and grow strong and wise for many a year. That is the amount of what Mr. Gliggins calls my 'profane library.' The other department, the sacred, is made up of one book in two volumes, my mother's Bible. I must confess the first volume, beautiful and holy as it is, has little charm for me. Perhaps I am cold, but why should I act the hypocrite like so many who do not love it yet, to run with the crowd, feign they do ? Mr. Gliggins declares that I lack the historic instinct. It may be so. The second volume is my constant friend. Without it how could I live and bear my task. In sickness and sorrow I open its golden pages and a healing spirit enters me, a soft warmth permeates my whole being, and I hear a voice bidding me quit weariness and sickness and come to the refreshing fountain which flows from my Lord. I am wandering from my begging expedition, which was to ask you for a few books, Dickens or Thackeray. Father had just a common-school education, and he cares little for poets of the Wordsworth stamp. Chaucer and Spenser I might read to him if he was troubled with insomnia and wanted a cure. I have read Scott until he knows him by heart. I read every night to father, for hours and hours. It eases his mind, banishes the past for a while at least, and saves so much murmuring and complaining. Father is not a philosopher, and hence is unable to take his troubles with equanimity. When he is alone, and this must be, as I have no magic wand to bring the groceries to my door, his time is passed in lamenting his lost wealth. You may not know that he was once the partner of Mr. Dixon, in fact the first promotor of that gentleman's plant. Well, Mr. Dixon attended strictly to business; so did papa as long as my mother lived. But a man of your long experience will agree with me, that there are women who pilot men to success. My dear mother was one of them. When she died, I was too young to notice business matters with any interest, but I have been told by Mr. Dixon that father's money went like water through a sieve. Being a man of imagination, he hatched a thousand foolish schemes; being a man of heart, he listened to the music of a goodly number of flatterers until they could hang to him no longer. Mr. Dixon tried to relieve him, but father was above advice; he saw honest men in the schemers, and a schemer in the honest man who has always been more than ready to help, without the slightest return, an old partner. Father saved little—just the few acres and the cottage, ground enough to give me exercise, with the furniture and a few books of my mother. For these things, though papa is too proud to say so, we have to thank our old friend Mr. Dixon. How thankful I am on father's account that we have a little home where he can grope around without bothering any one!"

"I am glad to know your tastes, Miss Croydon," said Père Monnier, "which I deem excellent. I prefer, however, that you come and inspect my library. Well known to me its every nook and cranny, but to a stranger a hopeless confusion."

Père Monnier laughed.

"You can browse and burrow there at your will. At home or abroad the library door will be open. Genevieve will be your willing guide. As the shelves run ceilingward, and as your climbing abilities may be limited, Napoleon and his step-ladder will solve the difficulty. He is an old soldier, and his great delight will be to have your ear while he tells of battles won. The lost are not palatable in the telling. Should you show interest you will gain his friendship at once and his grateful service. I have kept you from your pupils, so with a hope that Genevieve may give you no trouble, but much comfort, I will say good-by."

The Père slowly sauntered homewards. Miss Croydon, deputizing one of her pupils to ring the bell, entered the schoolroom and sat by her desk.

She had often heard of Père Monnier and his winning ways; for the first time she owned his spell. It was no wonder that this man-loving man should from his first coming strongly appeal to the rough people who eked out life in these mountain recesses. Experience had taught her that they were sharp in their judgment of character, and generally correct in it. Their estimate of Père Monnier was well taken; it was just; it was true. A simple, childlike man he was, whose long years of study and travel had not dried up the fountain of youth. He was ever young, that charm which few of us carry along with age. For his sake, his little ward should be cared for and well taught. What graciousness in throwing open his large and rare book-collection to one who was a stranger in race and creed, and what delight the library held for summer evenings and winter nights, delights for her poor blind father! Romance would make him forget and remember; forget present sorrows, remember past joys. A smile lit up her face; there was no drudgery associated with the day.

The bell rang, barely audible at first, then loud, jerky, and long, a pleasant occupation for the urchin who held it and who leaped and laughed to its noise.

The children stopped their games, some quickly and willingly, others slowly and surlily, and in bunches and as stragglers entered the schoolhouse and took their places. The hum began, and with it their school-work.

Their teacher's mood was sunny, and children, so apt in face-reading, carried the word to their homes that Père Monnier had visited the school and Miss Croydon by her face was well pleased.

Père Monnier's thoughts, as he entered his library, were of Genevieve and the future.

CHAPTER VI.

A PARTING.

"AND you are going away to live in the big city, Ruth, far from Squidville. I don't believe you will ever return. What shall I do without you? Just think of it! Seven years together and then to part."

The speaker was a girl of sixteen, whose arms were wildly thrown around her companion's neck.

They were standing in front of a little church, whose well-trimmed lawn was adorned with flowering shrubs and beds of flowers blending with every breeze in rich color.

"Oh, dear me, yes! Genevieve, I shall run up here once a year. It is ideal to pass a vacation in such a place. I shall enjoy it, I assure you, more than I do now. Distance lends enchantment to the view.

"Will it not be pleasant, Veev, to leave the smoky city and its din for home? for, after all, this being my birthplace must ever remain my home. There is another link, the strongest. In the little Methodist graveyard over yonder rests my mother, sleeping long years, and father but a few weeks. You must promise for my sake that now and then you will visit their graves and scatter a few flowers there. When your letter comes to me in my smoky den it will bear me away to where they lie, from the city's trouble and noise, to quiet and bliss."

"I shall not forget that, Ruth," said the tearful-eyed Genevieve. "You have done so much for me in these years. I was just thinking of the first day I went to your school. How proud were uncle and Napoleon and Anna! I remember you begging books, and how good you were that day, so good that the scholars wanted Père Monnier to make a visit every day. Don't you remember, Ruth?"

"Yes, I remember. It was my first meeting with your uncle. I had heard from Mr. Dixon so much about him that I was anxious to see him, and your first day was the long-looked-for opportunity. Mr. Dixon had told me that if he was in sorrow he would go at once to Père Monnier and unbosom himself. Such a speech coming from so close-mouthed a man as Mr. Dixon satisfied me that the Père was made of genuine stuff. I was ready to confess. I made no bones about telling my ills, and as the greatest was to keep my father in good humor, I had to bespeak a cure. Right royally it was given. The library was thrown open, and what consolation have I not carried out of that dear old room! When I am sad, in the big city you dread so much, I will shut my eyes and revisit Père Monnier's library. It is not the city, I assure you, that drives me from my old home and beloved friends. It is the commonplace desire to earn my own living, and a bit of thrift driven into me by long experience to be a busy little bee as yonder bright fellow tasting the sweets of the phlox, and lay up something to keep me out of the almshouse when the inevitable day comes that I can work no longer, and yet must await the night that ends all earthly work. I certainly should be as wise as the bee or the squirrel. How differently you are situated! No care; just live and laugh."

"But suppose uncle should die, Ruth, what then?"

"Such suppositions are foolish, Genevieve. Enjoy the mystic now. Sunshine is yours. Shadows and sorrows come soon enough. Just think of me, 'with a heart for any fate,' going to New York with a limited purse to achieve fortune. I don't know a single soul in that city. I know what is before me—loneliness, homesickness, but I shall conquer and rule them. It is childish to let such things defeat one's plans for the future. I am prepared to suffer, and in other years these sufferings will be sweet to recall. Suffering brings to the surface our best. I will let you know how things go. It will relieve my mind to sit down in my room and write page after page to Genevieve, recounting my chances and failures. I know how anxiously you will await these pages, how quickly you will tear the envelopes and run out amid these flower-beds to live over Ruth's struggles in the big city.

"You must promise me that just as soon as you have finished the last page you will be ready to grasp your pen and send all the news to the exile. Everything you write will be interesting. No matter how trivial you may think a bit of news, to Ruth it will be of importance and interest."

"I won't fail, Ruth. I will write so much that you will be tired reading and regret giving such instructions. I am sure that you will make friends soon and find work. You will then tire of news from here, and your letter will be reduced to a hurried sheet. Last year I was away visiting in Montreal, and I met so many people that I liked, and they liked me, and I promised to write to them, and I did, but they soon forgot, and now they are like a dream to me. You will meet so many nice people, and you will see so many beautiful things, and time will run so fast, that you can afford precious little of it to thoughts of these hills."

"You are cruel, Genevieve, to talk in that way. How could I dare to forget where so much of my life has been spent and where my parents lie sleeping? No, Genevieve; I shall not forget, and I know you will not, so let us seek Père Monnier. It will be hard to say good-by to him. His like I shall not easily find. I have a letter of recommendation from my own pastor, but one from the Père will be of great assistance. When all the ministers guarantee my character I ought to have little trouble in finding work."

"We will find uncle in the library. All his spare time is spent there. I wonder he never grows tired reading book after book. You can see his head through the window, the big blue pencil behind his ear. Now it's gone; he has met something, as he says, worth bagging. A blue mark is the shot with which he takes his game. I wonder how he keeps all those blue marks in his head. I am sure they would set me crazy. I don't think that women have such big heads to cram as men."

"It's not the bigness of the head, dear; it's brains, Genevieve. Your saying is not always correct. You meet men who have more brains than the women around them, and you meet women who have more brains than the men around them, and so it goes. There, the Père's eye has caught us. See how he laughs at your awfully serious face. Let us go to him."

With arms around each other's waists, teacher and pupil entered the well-known library. There were tears in the eyes of Ruth Croydon.

A Parting.

The library was a large room, two sides being shelved to the ceiling in fancy-wrought maple wood, done in the Père's leisure the first year of his coming to the parish. The two other sides of the room were converted into a picture-gallery. The pictures were as curiously mated as his books. A copy of Millet's "Angelus" had the place of honor, "because," said the Père to an inquirer, "the painter is my countryman and the scene familiar to my childhood. If I had only a bell on my church, any summer's eve I could almost produce the same scene in my parish. Sometimes I am lonesome—not often—everybody is. I suppose what makes it is that this country is not my native land; at least that has often been my thought. On such occasions I look at the picture. I see dear old France, the laughing yellow corn, the vine-clad hills. I hear the dear old purring river and the birds singing in the green hedges their little songs just before going to bed. Then over hill and vale I hear the great cathedral bell sweetly singing that wonderful song of love, 'The Angel of the Lord declared unto Mary: and she conceived of the Holy Ghost.' Jacques drops his fork and Rosalie her basket, then bending their heads in holy prayer, proclaim the prerogatives of Mary, while I meditate, dream, drift away, praying for His grace in my heart, that I, too, may one day participate in the Resurrection. When I awake the loneliness has gone and I feel a newer man, fresh, agreeable, willing to bear my little burdens in cheerfulness and to help those who struggle in gloom with bits of my own sunshine. I think that is sufficient explanation why the Barbison painter should have the place of honor."

Touching Millet's "Angelus" hung—strange the contrast!—Rosa Bonheur's "Scotch Raid."

"See," would Père Monnier say to his visitor, "what a talking picture this is, full of wild life, the darting gleam in the eyes, the toss of the nose, the strange huddling together! That's just as they must be."

The "Scotch Raid" had as its companion Raphael's "Madonna of the Chair," which was one of the treasures of Père Monnier, purchased in Florence during his student days, and religiously borne in all his wanderings until he became master of a house. Then the fitting of a library was his first work, and the first picture hung was his Madonna of the dreamy eyes and motherly expression.

There were other pictures: charming studies of his long-loved Venice by Fildes, bits by Troyon, Van Marcke, Charles Émile Jacques, and Jadin, showing their owner's love for animals, a love which had given him daily hours of delight. The lover of nature pines not for a companion in his rambles; his companions are everywhere when love has given him the eyes to see and the ears to hear. Here and there in the library, framed and hung on the walls, or unmounted and resting on the book-shelves, were magnificent views of the wild but picturesque scenery of the Adirondacks—mountains wooded to their base with the stately pine and the ragged-edged spruce; jutting hills of dull red sand-capped by mighty boulders; rivers lashing themselves into creamy whiteness against the glossy hard rocks; lovely lakes modestly hiding themselves in the depth of the woods, the seeker coming upon them by surprise; burly huntsmen, dogs and deer, all that made the Adirondacks a pleasant place to spin one's life away. Near the windows were palms, ferns, geraniums, and hibiscus, cunningly placed to bring out every speck of color. Two large cages contained a rare collection of canaries and linnets, whose morning songs were a mirthful awakening to the household, " much pleasanter," was Père Monnier's remark, " than Napoleon's old hand-bell, or the new alarm-clock," a Christmas gift from one of his parishioners who had wandered to the far West, yet wished to be kept in mind by his pastor. The huge St. Bernard lazily lying on a rug, opening his eye now and then, and stretching his paws, completed the picture of the library the morning Ruth Croydon entered it to bid her friend good-by.

It was a picture that often came to her mind in days long after when her thoughts wandered to Genevieve.

As they entered, Père Monnier laid down the book he held and arose to greet his visitors.

"Always reading, Père," was Ruth Croydon's greeting.

"Oh! no, Ruth, not always, but about every chance I have," smilingly responded the Père.

"I suppose, Père, that book is something very deep, to judge from your intentness. Genevieve and I were playing peep-through-the-window. It is a new book, I can tell that. I have spent so much time here that I know at least all the old ones either by name or by something peculiar to their covers."

"You are right, Ruth, this is a new book, new to me; a wonderful book written by one who abhors our present pettiness and lives in the greatness of the past. The man who wrote this book dwells on a mountain, serene but not cold. He sees into our littleness so keenly and wisely that he would not be harsh. Inexorable as his logic is, it is clothed in tenderness."

"You are, indeed, eloquent, Père, on this book. I am sorry I shall not have an opportunity to read it. I fear my reading days are over. When one has to work for a living there will be little time to educate the soul. How I shall miss this library! But we cannot have things as we will, and repining at our fate brings no cure. What is the name of the book, if I may ask?"

"The name of the book is 'Parochial Sermons,' by Dr. Newman."

"Well, I am afraid it would be too heavy for me. Yet if I were to remain I should have audacity enough to tackle it."

"And you would certainly master it, Ruth; you use your brains. You think for yourself, and for such a one Dr. Newman is simple. You are a great lover of style, a love in which I join. His style is orderly, grasping, tender, and vivid, as clear, calm, and lovely as one of our mountain lakes on a summer's day. His every pen-touch has a meaning. Each sentence is a mosaic laid with an eye to the ultimate end, which is a picture as chastely done as a Vatican Raphael."

"Well, some day I may return, perhaps to pass a vacation at my old home; then I shall borrow the book. I know from what you tell me it must be interesting."

"So you go away for good, Ruth?"

"Yes, Père, I go away, in the words of the old song, 'It may be for years and it may be forever.' Who can say? I was thinking to-day, just as I came to pay you my last visit, that I should love to meet a genuine witch who could answer that question. Alas! Père, witches and fairies are dead. The world has slaughtered imagination; dullards have touched every cranny and corner with their prosy stick, proclaiming that the strange world so wonderfully dear to my Saxon forefathers is, like everything else they write about, but dust, our century, impudent and audacious, scoffing and sneering at all time behind its august highness."

"I think you are slightly cynical, Ruth, this beautiful morning, your last on your native heath. Why should you follow your century in banishing the fairies? I have not much to say on the witch question. Salem superstition is surely something to be deplored, its riddance a good thing, but the laughing, merry, music-loving fairies in their hilarious ring-dances around the rowan-trees, why should they be banished? I fear we are banishing too much; our lives soon will be dull and prosy. I well remember when I was a child what pleasure tales of the fairies gave me. I was never weary listening to my grandfather. Since those days I own allegiance to the gentle, harmless little folk who haunt every nook and cranny of my native land. I love their historians and, strange as it may seem to you, Ruth, I can read about the little fellows with as much delight to-day as I listened to my grandfather in childhood's impressionable time. I can shut my eyes and hear their ringing whoop come over the hill, see the princely cavalcade led by their king on white horse come dashing through the glen—the fairy king, his merry men and ladies gay, all dressed in green and red.

How gracefully they sit on their steeds, and with what gallantry they alight at their goal, the red-berried rowan-tree! Then floats to me their music, dainty and delicious, as weird as that of Chopin when languorous passion tossed his fretful soul. The king extends his hand and bows, his queen coyly accepts, and three times three, as light as swallow skims a lake, they skim the rich green grass around the rowan. Then knights and ladies fall in step and dance to the dawn. *Voilà!* you see the things that amuse your country pastor. Every man and woman is king over one realm, and that is imagination. There, I hold, the cynic and scoffer have no rights. I keep that domain to myself, and when I am tired and weary therein I may wander, finding rest under the trees, and comfort lying on its greensward."

"Père Monnier, you will always be young. A man of your age believing in fairies and reading children's books! I see you in a new light."

"You pay me a great compliment, Ruth, when you tell me I am young and that I will always be so. I have discovered, then, what great men in all ages have vainly sought, the elixir of youth. I would it were so, but what eluded Ponce de Leon I cannot pride myself in possessing. Age will crush me as she crushes other men, but I would like to so manage my heart that to age's grinding operations it could always oppose a bit of youth. I know there are some who deem youth a foolish waste; these read life awry and are the wearying misanthropists whose falsities are a deadly poison. When you leave us, Ruth, books will be put in your hands preaching loudly the gloom of life; scenes of misery will be presented to your keen eyes; cries of despair will reach your ears. Then will youth be necessary as a stay, and what youth loves. These fine, calmly set mountains of ours, never wearied or sad, youthful and restful, whether wrapped in green, faded brown, or clad in their loose mantle of wintry snow; these rivers of ours, so boyish in their ways, now calm and contented, loitering by green meadows, strolling by woody heights, then with the life of youth, merrily shouting, jumping over rocks, and, as if delighted at their feats, laughingly flowing on in merry good-humor with themselves—these things will brace you if you keep young. Amid scenes and sights which are loathsome you can, by shutting your eyes, see our rivers and mountains, hear in our maples the robin's song, and live again in Arcady. 'But I must wake,' you say. It is true; but you will bless the golden moments spent in dreaming, for with your waking will come the courage to bear, and the helpful thought that this old world after all is not the hideous place it seems when viewed from a city. I can understand a lover of bricks being a cynic, a lover of nature never."

"I don't think, Père, that I could ever become a brick-lover. I have spent too many years in the country for that. I remember that some Latin poet said that one may change his skies but not his affections. That is my case exactly."

"Well, Ruth, I do hope that you will return rich some day, and I can paraphrase what the poet said to John Gilpin: 'May I be here to see.'"

"Of course you must be here to see, Père, and Genevieve and Napoleon and Anna, else the whole scheme would amount to nothing. Just think of this place without you! Nonsense! The play without Hamlet."

"But remember, Ruth," said Genevieve, "you always said that nobody can tell what will turn up. There may be many changes before your return; perhaps you will never return."

"Why, Veev! What use in being so solemn? I have assured you that there is a small plot which interests me deeply, that is enough to bring me back. I hope something will turn up for me. Like Micawber I am waiting, and, when it does, like Barkis, 'I'm willin'' to seize it. And yet I go not of my own accord. The trustees, as long as my father lived, believed that they were doing a bit of charity, keeping the old man off the rates, by allowing his daughter to toil for a few dollars a week. When my father died the charity ended. Anybody, that is the thought of country people, can teach a country school; so I was dismissed, and the daughter of a trustee put in my place. I tell you it's the way of the world, and, as father used to say: 'Let her go at that, and pop goes the weasel.'"

"Ah, Ruth," said Père Monnier, "you are a brave girl! You will make out, never fear. It's a long lane that has no turn. You remember Mr. Dixon's saying, that there is luck in every life, if we know how to use it. I know you will not throw yours away. There is a little something about which I would like to talk, and yet I don't know well how to begin. I suppose my best plan is to blurt it out. I want to say that your stock of money is not large, and you may not have work at once. It is not as easy as you may think to procure a situation in a large city. For every vacancy there is always a horde of applicants. It may take time, and the waiting will eat up your little stock. Now it is always a good thing to replenish your purse, and this can be done by sending a little note to Genevieve. And I insist that the note will come long before the purse is exhausted."

Just then the Angelus rang out, and the Père arose to pray. As its last note trembled and died away, the vigorous hand-bell-shaking of Anna announced that her long-planned and carefully prepared dinner "for poor Ruth's going," as she put it, was steaming on the table. The delicious odors entering the library whetted their appetites. They found their places in the dining-room, and, Napoleon being in a merry mood, the dinner-chat could not be dull. How often in years to come did Ruth think of this dinner! Père Monnier carving the huge, well-stuffed turkey, with laugh and quip and tickling story; Napoleon so argumentative, yet couching all his arguments in a rich old-world politeness, that could in nowise offend, ready to nail every point with a story; Anna carried to a third heaven by the Père's well-turned compliments to her dinner, or open-mouthed in wonder at his patience with that "loose-tongued, crack-brained, soldier-talking Napoleon;" Genevieve in all the loveliness of her girlhood grace, living in the light of her uncle's eyes, loving him as the king of men.

CHAPTER VII.

WINNING A WAY.

GENEVIEVE MONNIER walked sadly through the lawn humming a couplet and followed by her dogs. Two months had passed since Ruth Croydon bade her good-by and whispered in her ear: "Genevieve, my darling, you will have a letter in a few days. Just as soon as I am settled and have found time to buy a sheet of paper and a bottle of ink, I will write so much that I will weary you, but you must have patience with your old friend."

Genevieve had eagerly watched the mail but no tidings came from her absent friend. She was beginning to lose hope.

Ruth had for years been not only her gifted teacher, but the only friend to whom she attached herself outside of her home. She was her constant companion. The two girls had become like sisters, sharing each other's thoughts, and calling each other by pet names, that human way of love. The couplet ran :

"For the new has charms which the old has not,
And the stranger's face makes the friend's forgot."

From whence it came she was unable to say, and she was too young to trouble herself much; suffice it that it came at the right time and blended with her mood.

The dogs drew themselves towards their mistress cautiously and with pitying looks, as do the subjects of Eastern potentates, begging recognition. There is something in the fine, manly face of the St. Bernard that disarms anger. Genevieve dried her tears and looked kindly. The dogs, who read the human eye in a twinkle, went merry and ran to kiss and caress their mistress.

She allowed their mood, but paid no attention to their frolic. They quieted for a moment, listened with a comical-looking seriousness, and then went barking down the road to greet Napoleon on his return from the post-office.

"Any letters for me, Napoleon? You promised to bring me a fat one. I hope you keep your promises."

"Ah, Genevieve, old Napoleon says more than his prayers. Who would be writing to you? If I had thought you were so anxious, I would have written a letter myself."

"Have you the letter? I see you grinning. You are just fooling me. I will give you a good hug, and read you a new story about war if you stop your fooling and give me my letter."

"Bright Eyes, your offer is tempting, but how can Postmaster Buttons give out letters if they don't come in?"

"You are a rogue, Napoleon, you have a letter. I know by your eyes. That's the way uncle always knows when you are fooling."

"Those eyes of mine would hang me, Genevieve. Here's your letter. I'll warrant it's fat enough and worth waiting for. I was just having fun with you."

The laughing old soldier walked briskly away to deliver his master's mail, and Genevieve hastily tore open the bulging envelope and passionately kissed the letter.

"From Ruth, my good, dear Ruth it comes!" she exclaimed as she read snatches here and there, then folded it and ran to the kitchen where Anna, sighing and praying, was watching a mutton-roast.

Anna was astonished at Genevieve's dash. She forgot the roast to fondle her darling, and warn her to be careful and not run that way in future for fear of falling and perhaps laming herself for life.

"What put it in your head to come with such a run? You just took my breath away. Were you scared? I reckon you was; and a little bird whispered in my ear how it was. That silly Napoleon! I wonder the Père does not make him mind; he doesn't bother him, child, and the bad breeding is on him. Well, the bird said to me that silly Napoleon fooled around the grass until he caught a large frog, and when you asked him for a letter he showed you the frog, and that's what put fire to your toes."

"No, Anna; he did not do anything to me to-day, only torment me a little, and that's nothing."

"That's his nature, Genevieve. Well, would you think that a little bird would whisper lies? I'll never give it a crumb again."

"Oh! don't say that, Anna; maybe the poor little fellow was telling you about what happened a few days ago and you mistook it for to-day."

"I wouldn't wonder but I did. It's just like me to mix things; the older one's head grows the less room it has to keep new things fresh."

"I have a surprise for you, Anna—a letter from Ruth. I thought we would read it together while Napoleon is in the barn. I don't mind him hearing it, but he would tire us out asking questions."

"He would tire out Saint Peter, child, and a band of angels. Wait till I turn the meat and you can begin. I don't want to lose a word. If you meet high words, just make them small as you go along, the better for me to come at them. I know Ruth was good on the dictionary-book."

Anna rocked on her easy-chair, her eyes on the sweet-smelling roast, her ears ready to catch the longed-for news. Genevieve sat by her side and read:

"DEAR V.:

"What use to make apologies? I should have written long, long ago. I did not. It would take more sheets than I am at leisure to fill, to give you all my reasons. Some day, V., away up in our old home, under the cooling maples, I will tell you the whole tale; here I can give but a few things, enough, I think, to be taken as an apology for what you doubtless thought was hard-hearted indifference on my part. You remember, on that sorrowful day of my departure, the Père warning me that work was not so easy to find in the big city as the country-bred are wont to suppose. I found the truth of this statement my first week here. I met hundreds who were looking, like me, for something to turn up. I soon made their acquaintance. It was easy to do so, as misery is a most companionable fellow. From them I learned that work was scarce and workers plenty, a consequence which made labor cheap—mere bread-getting. Some of my companions in work-seeking had been idle for months, and the chances of getting employment at an early date are few. It makes me nervous to hear the tales of these people. In the dear old homestead we know nothing of poverty. If some one is needy his neighbors succor him. Then rent is cheap, every one owning his house, raising his potatoes, having his fuel, his milk, his butter, his eggs, his pork, while here the rent is high, the accommodations dirty-looking, cramped, and miserable. Everything must be bought at a high price; then it lacks the freshness and taste of the country. When work is plenty and pay good, the toiler subsists. Imagine his condition when he cannot find work! I should here remark that the country practice of running a store-bill when folks are out of work, and paying it when they are at work, would not be allowed here, and with good reason. In the country you can easily find your debtors; in the cities it would be the old story of finding grandmother's needle lost in a haystack. Honesty, although it is the best of policy, is not as widely diffused as we mountaineers think. We judge the rest of the world by ourselves.

"As soon as I arrived in New York I bought the morning papers, went to a hotel, and diligently conned the advertisements for two things. I wanted a room at a reasonable price and work. I found the room without any trouble, paying for it in advance. A month's rent for my room would hire a snug cottage at home. Let me describe the room, it won't take long. I begin with the largest piece of furniture in it, the bed—narrow, hard as a block, only restful when one is tired out tramping the streets. I cannot tell you what a weary feeling the city's pavements give to country legs. I have a little table, a bit loose—don't inquire into its age and color. If this letter is kind of shaky lay it to the table. I have a chair that must be used with caution, as one of its hind legs was crushed many moons ago, and since that unfortunate event the limb shows signs of bending under a pressure of a hundred pounds.

"You remember when Mr. Dixon weighed us your Ruth was a hundred and forty-five pounds. Although she keeps descending in the scale it is at a slow rate, so you can well understand why caution is necessary. I have a pitcher and a bowl and two worn-out old towels, that I keep where the landlady, a deserving woman struggling like myself to live, placed them. I use my own. I can barely turn in my room. I must not forget to describe the walls: they are papered; the color don't ask, for I am giving a truthful account, and if I tried to tell you the color I fear I would romance. It is a rainbow hue and more. The former dwellers, in their leisure moments, have done some decoration. Above my bed is a celebrated pacer, and a little way from him two ill-looking pugilists in the attitude of defence. Evidently the room was once occupied by an admirer of manly sports. The woman that vacated this room the day before I took possession had other tastes. She pictured a patch with paper dolls, much to the disgust of my landlady. I will leave no memento of my tastes. I have neither care nor leisure to do so. In truth, my landlady gave me a hint that she preferred the 'clean walls' to even the most artistic effects.

Having been a school-teacher, I know the necessity of obedience. Here's a secret. When I left home I brought with me a slip of a fuchsia from a plant that my poor mother grew. I wanted to have a green bit of the old home around me. I cannot tell you how many rags I wrapped around that slip, and the care with which I laid it in the bottom of my trunk. I was overjoyed that the train-jostle and rough portering had not disturbed my little fellow. Like a bird in his nest of batting he lay. I gave an urchin a few cents to fill a tomato-canister with clay. He was quick to inform me that it was no easy job, and a look from my window convinced me of the truth of the youngster's opinion.

"I set with many a prayer and hope my slip in the canister, but its growth is slow; it seems to mourn for its mother and the mountains.

"Now, Veev, you have an idea of Ruth's room. The house is made up of such rooms. As to the inhabitants, I know little of them, and they return my phrase. Every morning I sit by my window and watch them hurry to work—pale, shrivelled-skinned, sad-faced men and women, bowing and bending, sickly like plants shut out from air and sun. In the women I am continually noting the dulness of the eyes and the haggard motion of their bodies. What a sorry set they would make in Squidville! You would look on them as people from some low-civilized new land, not as the bread-earners from the capital of the world's democracy. The heartlessness with which these poor creatures are made to toil for a mere pittance in shops and factories that are even viler than their miserable homes rouses my anger and makes me ask what, after all, has our boasted democracy done for the poor. All its laws are for the rich; 'wealth accumulates and men decay.'

"The other evening I saw a miserable old woman huddled on a corner of Fifth Avenue—that street of all kinds of blood, now, thanks to fat purses, reckoned blue—playing an old hand-organ. You would hardly guess the tune; it was Strauss' 'Blue Danube.' I dropped a few cents into the old tin pan that lay by her side, and we fell into conversation. She told me that her husband, a worthless fellow, had died a few years ago, and when rheumatism crippled her so that she could no longer wash and scrub for a living, a good gentleman named O'Connor bought her the organ and paid her room-rent. This gentleman I had occasion to meet since my chat with the old woman. She calls herself old Sal, and in my life I never before met with such a vitriol tongue set loose against society. If men and women of her condition are so desperately preaching against a form of government which, they will tell you, by its laws made at the will of the rich man's pocket-book, makes them yearly more miserable and degraded, what may we not expect in the future? Of this unrest of the clamoring masses, bent, broken, bleeding humanity, suspicious of government and of churches, we mountaineers know nothing. Old Sal was a revolutionist. She wanted smash, and her sole prayer seemed to be that she would live to have a hand in it. She told me many stories of hardship, one in particular having eaten into her marrow. It seems that a mother died and left a little girl. Old Sal (there is in the wrinkled old dame a great deal of the milk of human kindness) took the child, as she says, 'under her wing,' but the very day of the mother's death Sal and the child were thrown out in the street by the house-owner, 'a prayer-and-preaching man called Fortune,' to cite Sal's cynical phrase. I know the Père would love to meet Sal.

"Now, to matters more personal. I tried for weeks to find a place. I went from office to office in search of work. Employers were very sorry that they had at present nothing in my line, but they would take my name and my address. I was to be Micawber; when the something turned up I was to be notified. This is a polite mode of saying: 'Don't trouble us any more.' At first it is kind of soothing to the new-comer, but when he finds it is the common stock-in-trade it palls and finally stupefies him.

"I walked the soles off my mountain-boots in search of work, but it eluded me. My purse was nearly empty and something had to be done. Pride kept me in the city. Old Sal had told me so much about Mr. O'Connor that I made up my mind I would ask him for some position on his paper; anything would be welcome. I went down town one night, had the office pointed out by an urchin who was sleepily selling extras, and clambered up three flights of narrow dark stairs to a lighted corridor. On one of the doors I read 'Editorial Office. No Admittance.' An officious fellow came running to tell me that I must not enter the forbidden sanctum. I had no time for his lying tale. I pushed open the door and entered, just a little bit bewildered. Behind the desk filled with scraps and letters sat a gentleman. Yes, a gentleman. There was that indescribable something in the face which told me so. He arose quietly, and coming from his desk, handed me a chair and bade me be seated.

"I frankly told him my story. I suppose mine is not the first of the kind that he has heard, but he listened graciously, and when I was done he asked, in the softest of voices: 'Miss Croydon, what newspaper work could you do?' I could only answer: 'I don't know, but give me a chance.' 'Try something,' said Mr. O'Connor, 'for our Sunday edition, a poem, a tale, whatever you think you can do best, and bring it to me. In the mean time I will see what can be done.'

"My heart felt light. I went down the stairs and out into the cold night air with the speed of our deer. 'What shall I write?' asked I, a thousand times, that night on my homeward journey.

"In my own room the thought came that old Sal's story was better than any of mine, so I told it with all my ability. I took it to Mr. O'Connor, and watched his eyes for a sparkle of hope. I was not disappointed. His eyes seemed well pleased, and they were only striking the time of his heart.

"'Very well done, Miss Croydon; a strange tale. We must change the names of the characters. You can write readable matter, and that's what a newspaper wants. I will give you a note to the cashier, and you will have your pay at once. I think that in a few weeks I will be able to give you steady employment. Yes, no doubt of it. In the mean time, I will accept whatever you turn out. As you will have leisure I will ask you to accept a little book of mine, "Tales of a Court," written years ago. It may amuse you. I value it for bringing me here.'

"V., what was my astonishment to find the first story to be founded, as mine, on old Sal's tale! I am waiting for steady employment, then I shall move to better quarters and put by enough to allow a merry vacation with you, the Père, Anna, Napoleon, and the dogs. This is a rambling letter, but it is the only kind your Ruth is capable of writing. As soon as I post this I shall hurry to old Sal and drop something into her pan. The tale is hers; the telling mine. Tell the Père that I will send him the 'Tales of a Court,' and say to Anna I have a new recipe for sweetbread, and whisper in Napoleon's ears that his dogs beat anything in this city. Tell dear old Buttons to keep an eye on the homestead. 'Lots of commands,' I hear you saying, but remember, V., commanding was long my business. I was once a country schoolmistress.

"It is now midnight, and the faint roar of the city is dying out; the lights are yet bright, and the streets full of people; it is time for my weary head to seek the pillow. I'll woo sleep and dream of my Genevieve and the old home.

"RUTH CROYDON."

Tears were running down Anna's cheeks, and Genevieve's voice was choking.

"A terrible place the city is. It will fairly kill poor Miss Croydon," said Anna, rising to take from the oven her well-done roast.

"Wasn't she awfully brave, Anna," said Genevieve, "to go out at night to seek work? I wonder she was not afraid. I should die of fear. That Mr. O'Connor must be a good man, a very good man; but, Anna, who could be hard-hearted to Ruth?"

"Bless your wits, child, there's people that could

be hard-hearted to Saint Peter. If you only heard Napoleon tell how wild the folks can be, you wouldn't be talking as you do. While you were reading about Mr. O'Connor, I was thinking that that was the name of a man you were clean daft about when you first came here. You forget all the folk you knew before you came here, dear. How could you keep them in your head? Anyway, no need; those who were good to you will have their reward. Here comes Napoleon on a trot. Just as well put the letter away and give him the news by degrees, or else he'll clatter it all out in the post-office. From there it will run all over the town on wheels."

Anna wiped her eyes with her apron and looked cross as Napoleon entered the door.

CHAPTER VIII.

THE LAST GLIMPSE OF ERIN.

STRANORLAR is a sleepy little village in Donegal, the most northern of Irish counties. This village lies along the banks of one of those little Irish rivers which are always cheery and songful. The richest man in the town was Egbert Brown, a farmer and cattle-dealer. He was an obliging and kind-hearted man, and his neighbors, to show their appreciation of these qualities, had for many years appointed him as their representative to carry out the Poor Law. This gave him the pleasure of writing P. L. G. immediately after his name, which caused him to be addressed as Mr. Poor Law Guardian, a title that pleased him far more than "Mr. Brown." Of him, as of his race, it might be truly said, they dearly love a title. His duties as Guardian brought him to council with his fellows, every Monday morning, in a large brick building at the end of the town, known as the Poorhouse. This building was gloomy and ill-looking, and the rough and poorly plastered wall that surrounded it but added to its ugliness. Removed from this was another building called the Fever-house, equally forbidding, and still beyond the old bog, where paupers, their weary battles over, slept their last sweet sleep. These buildings were an eyesore to the peasantry, and few of them passed without crossing themselves and praying earnestly to God that "they or theirs," so ran the homely phrase, "would never be in want of such a place." Around their turf-fires the stranger heard many tales of the ghosts that journeyed each night from the old bog, to aimlessly wander through the corridors of the poorhouse until the first streaks of the dawn hurried them back into their narrow graves.

A part of this poorhouse was alloted to foundling children, and that curious Irish custom of giving the waif the name of the place where it is found made this part of the house interesting from its singular collection of names. Not a few of these waifs in after-years pleasantly called themselves Scotch-Irish.

On a certain cold, wintry Monday morning the Board adjourned, and Mr. Brown, in a hurry to make his usual inspection, was arrested by the smiling matron carrying a bundle.

"What have you there?" asked the Guardian, that no hurry could make impolite.

"A little bit of a tot, Mr. Brown, that a laborer found in your lime-kiln last night. It's a wonder he wasn't perished. He's so plump and fresh that I hate to saddle on him such a horrid name as Lime-kiln. I want you to give him something less heavy, a bit lighter to carry."

"Well, now," said Mr. Brown, pulling his beard and looking as if in a brown-study, "matron, you have put me in a new position."

"Ah," said the matron slyly, "Mr. Brown, you fill all positions admirably!"

"Matron, don't flatter me. As you tell me he was fortunate in not being frozen or chilled to death, why not call him Fortune?" and Mr. Brown laughed loud.

"Fortune!" exclaimed the matron. "What a happy thought, Mr. Brown! Fortune shall be his name, and I hope there is a good fortune in store for him."

"I hope so. Indeed it is the least I wish the youngster." And Mr. Brown hurried on where duty called.

From that day on he took an interest in the child, an interest which took the form of asking the matron every Monday: "And the child is having good fortune?"

The matron's cheery reply, "Good fortune, Mr. Brown," provoked a little quiet laugh only known in his eyes. The child grew fair of features and lively of disposition. At the age of fifteen, an application tendered the Guardians for a strong, healthy boy, limb-sound and work-willing, was accepted, and after a long debate James Fortune was chosen as the most fitting to fill the conditions. The debate was a child's rattle, as most official din is.

The Guardians cared little for waif-going or waif-coming, but no opportunity was allowed to pass where, like all officialism, they could be charmed with their own mouth-music. Egbert Brown was silent during this shopkeepers' din presided over by an impecunious and rack-renting lord. When it was done, Mr. Brown quietly remarked that he might like to have the youth himself, as he had the best right; at least that was his thought. The boy was found in his lime-kiln when a few days old and he, Mr. Brown, had given him the euphonious name which he now bore.

"What a joker!" said a long, lean shopkeeper, whose reluctant debtors had made him a P. L. G. "Mr. Brown is one of the wittiest men I have ever met." The lord, with a sneer for the long, lean talker, ordered the boy to be given to Mr. Brown. At his command there was a bowing of heads. Even Mr. Kinfy, the Radical, and Owen Cunliffe, the ardent Home-Ruler, were overmastered with delight when Lord Daffadowndilly threw them a leering wink. Mr. Brown thanked his lordship in that flattery which is a product of lands where centuries have known but two classes, the oppressors and the oppressed.

That Monday Mr. Brown briskly walked home

with his charge and presented the pretty boy in girl's clothes to his wife, who was, to say the least, not over-kindly bent to Poorhouse trash. She was obedient, however, to her husband, a gift getting rarer and much to be loved in a woman, and so her nimble fingers, from a many years' old clothes' assortment of her husband, fitted James Fortune's first manly garment. She was proud of her own industry and hence had no doubt of the boy's good looks, which she openly avowed, more to please her handiwork than to give great mother Nature credit.

The boy was as docile as a pet dog, and set himself to please his mistress and earn a smile with all the diligence in him. The name of Brown carried terror to his heart. From his earliest recollection it meant superiority, importance. Whenever, later, he could register a thought it was the thought of the altitude of Mr. Brown in his fine black clothes over the bowing and cringing paupers in their Irish flannels and foreign corduroys.

Mrs. Brown was pleased with his willingness, but formed her face sour and her tongue tart "to keep him," as she said, "in his place," that place being on the same level with her collie—at her bid and beck. Young Fortune, whose life had been set to the music of command, heeded well the ways of Mrs. Brown. The born slave rarely chafes at his condition. His promptness pleased his master. To keep in mind his servitude, Mrs. Brown, in the presence of her husband, putting forth a plea of the boy's stupidity, would box his ears, and the boy, recognizing this as part of Mrs. Brown's official duties, went through it uncomplainingly. There was one threat that made him wince, tremble at the knees, and spurt a tear— that threat was to send him back to the poorhouse. The thought of the cold walls, the corridors full of ghosts, the trembling old men all huddled together, their queer tam-o-shanter caps, the beetle-browed officials, the old bog, his gingham girl's clothes, unnerved and sickened him. He had a taste for reading, and now and then would hide a piece of paper to read in the early morning before the shrill voice of his mistress brought him from the garret to the body of the house. As Mrs. Brown's theory was that book-reading spoils servants, the boy was never permitted to be tempted. The bookcase was always locked. When Mrs. Brown was away visiting, the lad was accustomed to find pleasure in reading the names of the books through the glass. The slightest footfall made him jump, grasp his duster, and assume the attitude of servitude.

He grew strong, cast off the poorhouse pallor for bubbling health. His eyes, light gray, lost their sleepy look and became sparkling and laughter-suggesting; his wan cheeks became Irish-rosy-red, a color no flesh takes in our clime. At the age of seventeen Mr. Brown called him a man, and to men's work he went, glad to get away from the observant eye of Mrs. Brown.

He was taught to plough, harrow, sow the seed, and thus save his master the cotter's expenses. One day, while he was ploughing, he saw a band of young and old coming his way. The young were laughing and singing, the old weeping. The sight was new to him, and fired with curiosity he left his horses to nip the few grass-shoots within their reach and joined the band, who at his request sat down under the shade of a few sycamores to take an early mid-day meal.

"What's up, boys?" he cried. "Where are you going, and what are some of you old folks crying about?" The young shouted, "We are off to America," and the old, "Our boys and girls are leaving us, never to see us any more. Why shouldn't we cry?"

James Fortune was bewildered. After their departure but one word, "America," was ever in his ears.

He watched them until he could see them no longer; then, from some impulse he could not understand, he sat down and cried bitterly.

"You did not, James, do much ploughing to-day. Were you sick?" said Mr. Brown, who made a daily inspection of his farm.

"Yes, sir," was the reply. "I was a kind of lonesome, not feeling well."

"James, you must do your work," said the master,

"and not idle away your time, else I may have to return you to the poorhouse."

"Mr. Brown," said the mistress, "you are entirely too soft, unfitted to handle this poorhouse trash. Some of these days the lazy brat will turn his tongue on you and give you pay for your kindness. A flogging would do him good, and I am sure one of the constabulary would oblige us."

"James," continued Mr. Brown, "this must not happen again. I fear you were idling away your time with those lazy villains that went to-day to Donegal to take passage for America. The quicker the country is rid of these Papists the better. I heard the last boat-load of these people that left all died like a lot of dogs with ship-fever. Served them right. Yes, we must give thanks to God that they are quietly leaving the country. If they continue going at this rate grazing will soon be cheap. James, James, how happy you should be! Just compare your lot to those emigrants that will have to be packed in the ship as tight as you have seen herrings in the last barrel I bought, and then the ship, an old tub of a thing, will in all probability go to the bottom even if she manages to keep afloat until they board her. Even if she crosses they will be all dead of the fever. Some day I will read you about their sufferings from an American paper sent to me by a boyhood friend. Then you will bless your stars that you have such a home; indeed, foolish boy, you will."

Mr. Brown dismissed the boy, who morosely sought his lonesome garret muttering "America." That night he dreamt of ships sailing away from Donegal, full of life and gayety, over seas to a land of milk and honey. He could see gold and silver scattered everywhere. He awoke while picking up these precious metals. Mrs. Brown's voice swept his garret, and, astonished that he no longer feared it, was soon about his daily tasks.

The Browns noted a strangeness growing over him, but they diagnosed it as fear of losing his home, and so the boy was mercifully spared their lectures.

Nearly a year after the emigrants' sailing, while he was engaged in dusting, he found lying in an easy-chair a paper which to his delight turned out to be *The American Eagle*. His heart beat wildly; the find was more precious than gold. He folded it carefully, opened his jacket and shirt, and placed it inside, dancing the meanwhile from pure joy.

"Take the cows this morning to the holms," said Mr. Brown. "I am going away for a few days, and, my young man, see that there are no complaints against you when I return, else you are handed over to those that will take a strap and lighten your gait. Do nothing unless you ask your mistress' permission."

The cows, large, well-fed, and sleek, were soon sauntering slowly along the narrow lane that led to the holms. As soon as the lad was out of sight of the house he unbuttoned his jacket and pulled out his treasure and commenced reading. When the holms were reached, he threw himself on a primrose bed by the river's side, right under the morning song of a lark, and in a half-doze dreamt for hours, then arose, jumped about like a lamb intoxicated with spring, shouting " America ! "

He was aroused by a noise. Was it the little babbling river that prattled at his feet? He listened. It was a human voice. Louder it came. He knew it too well. It was the shrill shriek of his mistress threatening the stick. A moment's thought and his shoes were off, his trousers rolled up. Mrs. Brown was hurrying on. James Fortune waded the stream and hid behind a clump of sally-bushes, listening to her excited talk.

" If I find you, you young villain, I'll give you the stick in a way that will bring you to your senses, you evil-doer ! I will thrash you within an inch of your life, you brat ! It's well seen your master is away. Serves him right, when he so forgot himself as to bring poorhouse trash under my roof. If I was only at your ear, I'll warrant the pull I would give it would make you hear very lively. Jamie ! Jamie, I say ! "

To her call there came no sound save the little river's babble and the lark's song. Seeing her efforts useless to recall the truant boy, she returned home vowing vengeance on his head.

From behind the clump of sallies he watched her discomfiture with keen delight. As she passed from his sight he arose and, kissing his hand in her direction, followed the river bank until he had reached the highway that led to Donegal town. Mounting a stone fence he could see the red brick walls of the poorhouse, beyond them the dreaded fever-house, while his imagination quickly supplied the dreaded old bog.

A chill ran through him; he trembled, and almost fell from his heights. "I hope you'll burn up some day," he hissed like a snake crossed in its path. "When I get rich one of these days, I'll come back and make myself a Guardian. No, I won't, either. I'll never come back. Whatever would bring me back? Who cares for me? Who has ever done anything for me? Then it would be always cast up in my face that I was a poorhouse brat, a pauper. I won't come back. I'll die first. I'll go to America. I see by the paper that everybody can get work there—whole pages about men wanted. Over there nobody will know me, and I will just be as well treated as if I had a father and mother. I'm going." Just then looking in another direction he caught a glimpse of the Brown homestead, a glimpse that curled his lip and made him jump from the stone fence. "I'll never see you again," he cried, "never! never! I'll die first. Oh! how I hate you!" And thus, muttering to himself, he started on a run on the road that led to Donegal. Soon his run was changed to a steady, brisk walk, and his face put on a rough determination that had never been there before. Now and then he threw a glance over his shoulder to see if the Browns were in pursuit, then chided his foolish fears. A night would pass before he would be sought, and by that time he hoped to be in the little seaport town, and, perhaps, the next day he would be on the ocean sailing to the land of promise, work, and happiness.

He continued walking until the night set in and aroused his sleeping ghost and fairy tales to life. To arrest his fears he whistled, held down his head, tried to forget all the stories he had heard the old paupers relate when in the long summer evenings they sat behind the ivy-clad walls retelling the tales their fathers told in those long-gone happy days.

So he went on fearing and hoping until daylight soothed his pain by throwing a soft light over the hills, awakening the sheep, and calling forth a hymn from her spirit-bird the lark. There were no houses in sight, and being tired, more from battling with his fears than from physical exertion, he sought a bed near the road in the long green grass. A few hours would refresh him, and five or six hours' good walking would surely bring him to his destination. He was soon asleep. Youth requires no sleeping-potion to lull to rest. He awoke with a jump and shouted, as was his wont: "I'll be down at once, ma'am; I'm up!" then rubbing his eyes and looking around he laughed heartily at his mistake.

"No; it's not the Browns I hear," he said, "but it's somebody coming my way, so I'll take a look at them, and let them pass if they might be dangerous to me. But it's singing, they are, and its 'O'Donnel Abu' they're at."

His voice joined with theirs in the spirited refrain of the famous march:

"Wildly o'er Desmond the war-wolf is howling,
   Fearless the eagle sweeps over the plain,
The fox in the streets of the city is prowling—
   All, all who would scare them are banished or slain!
     Grasp, every stalwart hand,
     Hackbut and battle-brand—
Pay them all back the deep debt so long due!
     Norris and Clifford well
     Can of Tyrconnel tell.
Onward to glory! O'Donnel abu:

Sacred the cause that Clan-Connaill's defending—
   The altars we kneel at, and homes of our sires:
Ruthless the ruin the foe is extending—
   Midnight is red with the plunderer's fires!
     On with O'Donnel, then!
     Fight the old fight again,

> Sons of Tyrconnel, all valiant and true!
> Make the false Saxon feel
> Erin's avenging steel!
> Strike for your country! O'Donnel abu!"

Soon the singers came in sight, a band of young and old, similar to the one he had seen and talked with when ploughing Brown's farm. His heart beat high, he jumped from his hiding-place and ran to meet them, shouting like one witless: "I'm for Donegal! I'm for America! I'm going too!"

"God's blessing be about you wherever you go, poor boy!" said one of the elders as he marched beside his own fair boy, now and then looking into his fresh young face.

"Here's a 'capper' of bread and butter," said a rosy-faced girl, as she handed him two large slices of oaten bread thickly buttered. "You might be a bit hungry. Eat it. Anyway it won't do you any harm."

"I think I once saw you," said a third, "over at Brown's, and heard he had got you at the poorhouse. You look like the same boy. You're not running off with yourself and leaving old Brown fiddle for you? It kind a-looks like it."

The boy bit his lips at the mention of the poorhouse, feeling disgraced. He was wondering what to answer and if there was not some place where he would not be known as a poorhouse boy, when the girl that gave the bread whispered in his ear: "You did well to run away. If the Browns come after you, we'll give them a warm welcome. Don't feel bad. I have a box full of everything, and I'll divide and so will the rest. You won't want as long as we have a crumb between us. It was not your fault that you were in the poorhouse. I suppose it was the same old trick. The landlords (never mind, we'll come back some day and turn 'em out) threw your folk out and turned the land to grazing. Where else could you go?"

James Fortune's tongue was loosened. A woman's tongue had banished his shame and awkwardness.

"Yes, I did run away. I am not ashamed, either. The Browns thrashed me all the time, because I was an orphan; and that's the reason, too, I was in the poorhouse. I'll die before I go back! I hate the Browns! The Browns don't like you, neither; indeed they don't. When some of you passed one day going to America, just as you are now, he called you Papists, and was saying that it was good riddance to the country, and there would be cheap grazing. That's Brown for you, from his head to his toes."

That speech, awkwardly put, won his way to their hearts. He was one of them, a sufferer. They were bound to him by ties dear to the Irish heart. They became his protectors and pledged their word to bring him to a new land, where they firmly believed there was neither pain nor care—a land that held many of their brethren and of which they spoke around their blazing peat-fires much as the Jews, in their camps, must have talked of their Promised Land.

The little seaport town that they entered during the dinner hour was full of bustle and business. It happened to be a market-day, and this added to the general crowd that came as a convoy to see the sailing of the emigrants.

A man in a cockade and rainbow-colored dress blew a tin horn. James Fortune jostled the crowd to follow his first hero seen outside his dreams.

"Make way," said the hero. "Make way!" shouted the hero-worshipper. "We'll see something now."

The crowd—and what crowd in fun-loving equals an Irish crowd?—separated, giving the showman his asked-for space. The open, hard ground was soon covered by a piece of rug, and the showman, like all of his craft, loving his own speech, made a humorous address, feathering it with pointed allusions to the wrongs of Ireland "and the brave boys and girls around him who had to ship from the old land on account of these wrongs." These allusions branded him as a patriot and gained a cheerful audience. Then he tumbled, told jokes that brought roars of laughter, and, before passing round his hat, sang them a few verses which were wildly applauded—

verses that filled his cockade with pennies. The emigrants joined him in his song, and even a policeman's lips were seen to go.

"Adieu to Ballyshannon, where I was bred and born!
　Go where I may I'll think of you, as sure as night and morn:
　The kindly spot, the friendly town, where every one is known,
　And not a face in all the place but partly seems my own;
　There's not a house or window, there's not a field or hill,
　But east or west, in foreign lands, I'll recollect them still.
　I leave my warm heart with you, though back I'm forced to turn.
　So adieu to Ballyshannon and the winding banks of Erne!

"Adieu to evening dances where merry neighbors meet,
　And the fiddle says to the boys and girls, 'Get up and shake your feet!'
　To Shanacus and wise old talk of Erin's days gone by,
　Who trenched the rath on such a hill, and where the bones do lie
　Of saint, or king, or warrior chief, with tales of fairy power,
　And tender ditties sweetly sung to pass the twilight hour.
　The mournful song of exile is now for me to learn.
　Adieu my dear companions on the winding banks of Erne!

"If ever I'm a moneyed man, I mean, please God, to cast
　My golden anchor in the place where youthful years were passed.
　Though heads that now are black or brown must meanwhile gather gray,
　New faces rise by every hearth, and old ones drop away,
　Yet dearer still that Irish hill than all the world beside—
　It's home, sweet home, where'er I roam, through lands and waters wide;
　And if the Lord allows me, I surely will return
　To my native Ballyshannon and the winding banks of Erne."

When the showman withdrew, the lad idly and sorrowfully hung around the many booths that add to the jollity of a country fair.

By one booth, much frequented by the emigrants, he spent the most of his evening, looking every few minutes up and down the street to see if his painted hero would come forth from the public-house wherein he was fêted by the country folk, singing songs that gave them a temporary consolation for the quickly coming loss of boys and girls that were to them as the apple of their eye. This booth was kept by a sunny-faced old man, dressed in neat black. He had a word and a hand for everybody, knew every man, woman, and child at the fair, and spoke in English or rich, sonorous Gaelic, preferring the latter. His booth, like himself, was clean and tasteful, and was called " Malachy McCrudden's Standing "—a sign that swung from his tent-pole merely from custom, for the booth needed no such advertisement. It was the common talk that he had been a " spoiled priest," one who had studied the classics, went to Maynooth, but, having no clerical calling, returned home. In Ireland such men are looked upon with mingled respect and pity.

Malachy had to live, so he took to peddling religious books and pictures, first carrying a small pack, then his fortune rising, purchasing a donkey, and so on, until he now owned a sleek, well-fed pair of grays, noted on the road for their quick step and jaunty airs. Whatever his fortune was, no one but heartily wished that it might be doubled; but of this there was little fear, as the open-handed generosity of the man was a lasting check. It was his great sorrow to witness the monthly sailing of the best blood of his land, and to see their ancestral lands turned into sheep-pasture. "Scotch shepherds and collies," he would sadly say, "rule now, and my people are weary wanderers striving to make a home in the new land."

Malachy for many years performed, as the peasantry put it, the "last duty," and a sad and solemn duty it was—that of leading the last prayer on Irish earth. Before the ship sailed, the emigrants and their friends knelt down on the green Irish sod, in hearing of the rustling yellow corn that would be ground for the alien and stranger—knelt under the gray Irish sky, larks dropping their music the while, the murmuring ocean, that stretches so far from fatherland, at their feet, and, led by the deep, rich voice of Malachy, prayed for peace in this the hour of affliction for gray-haired and broken-hearted parents; for good crops on the mountain patches—a miracle, but God is powerful; for a fair voyage over the troublous-looking sea; for strong winds; for a safe arrival in port; for health, and, above all, that none of their bodies should wither and grow white in the caverns of the deep. The leadership of this last prayer had made the name of Malachy McCrudden a household word, and no boy or girl would think of leaving Ireland without taking with them some article bought at his stand. This was the reason why his booth was surrounded, some buying a prayer-book, some a little cross, others religious pictures, all receiving advice, and not a few of the girls receiving a few shillings slipped into their hands " for luck and on account of their decent fathers and mothers."

Malachy was not slow to notice the rough country lad in the ill-fitting clothes, that hung around his " stand " watching eagerly the buyers purchase, but buying nothing. He had seen, too, young Sally Kerrigan, who was going to Connecticut to join a brother, step up and give him a large slice of buttered bread, saying in her girlish way, " I only gave you a little bit before; take this, and when you want more come to me. I'll be over in the house that the showman's in, right forninst your eyes."

Towards evening, when the crowd became more scattered, Malachy found his opportunity to examine the boy.

" Are you from these parts, youngster ? " asked the peddler.

" From beyond the mountains," was the answer.

" And where are you bound for ? "

The boy smiled. " I am for America, sir, if there be any finding it and I can make my way to it."

" The ship sails early to-morrow morning, and I trust there is no fear of her not landing, as she is a likely craft," said Malachy.

"I hope I'll be with her," said the seemingly listless boy.

"Hope! Have you not your ticket? That's necessary before you can put your feet on the gang-plank. If you think of working your passage over I'm afraid you will be left, for the captain told me to-day that he would take nobody that was not able to pay either right down, or give security on animals and crops. The captain is a tough old customer. What he says you can depend on, you can rest your mind on that; there'll be no stowaways on this trip."

"Well, then, I suppose I'll have to go back. But it's only my body they'll be bringing." And reeking tears hurried down James Fortune's rosy cheeks.

"Don't cry, man, but just tell old Malachy how you are fixed—all about you. He may be able to do something for you, as he and the captain are purty thick."

"I am from Stranorlar," mumbled the boy. "I'm an orphan from the poorhouse, and the Browns took me and abused me, so I saw folks going to America and I said to myself, 'I'll be one of them,' so here I be. I met all these people around, and they said they would take me, too; but I don't know what to do; not a bit of me does. I cannot go if the captain is against it, for I can't fly, and I suppose Mr. Brown and the police will soon be upon me, so I'm done for."

"So you want to go to America like all the rest of them; fly away from misfortune, and I cannot blame you. Stay around here awhile. I will soon close my 'standing,' and then you and I can go and have a bite to eat and lay plans, perhaps see the captain, and have a little confab of our own. You must keep quiet and let no one know your business. Wherever you go, be sure to think much and speak little, and there will be no fear of your not getting along."

James Fortune's fears fled listening to Malachy. He had no longer any doubts of seeing the land of his dreams and hopes. He wandered aimlessly about from booth to booth, noting the strange things that met his eye. Hearing the showman's horn and seeing the running crowd, he was on the point of joining them when Malachy pulled his coat-tail and bade him follow.

In a few minutes' walk they were at the end of the town, before a comfortably thatched cottage surrounded with a tasteful stone fence. The enclosure was abloom with flowers that the owner, Captain Campbell, was said to have brought from strange lands. The captain, a grizzled sea-dog nearing the sixties, sat in front of the door fondling his grandchild and puffing steadily a curious old Dutch pipe whose long stem was a constant source of wonder to the peasantry, whose tastes ran to small bowls and short stems.

"How goes it, Captain Campbell?"

"Why, Malachy, man! come in and smoke a genuine American cigar given me by—you couldn't guess whom, man—by Jamie McDade. You know he always liked his drop, so when he went over there he took to selling it, and faith made out. He's rich, and growing more so every day. You can meet nearly everybody from these parts in his place. You were the first man he asked for, and the last one."

"Captain," said Malachy, passing the old sea-dog's compliment with a smile, "this is a poor boy who wants, like all the rest, to go to America. His money-bag is very small. He could pay half and work the rest if there would be a chance that way. He's an orphan boy, captain, and you should not be too hard upon him."

"Well, Malachy, I know this is coming out of your pocket entirely, so I will not be too hard on you. I'll take him, but he'll be the last—him and that showman. I'm taking the showman along on account of his antics. I expect him to keep the boys and girls alive during the crossing."

At the mention of the showman's name James Fortune's eyes danced with joy. Luck was in his way: the hero was to be his companion for weeks.

"What time, captain, will the *Blackbird* sail tomorrow?"

"At daylight, Malachy, or as soon after as we can. It might save you lots of trouble to get rid of the boy at once, so go down and tell the mate, Cassidy, that I said he is a crew-hand and to give him something light. Good-by, Malachy. When you're at the praying to-morrow, give us a small one for a stiff breeze. I'll try and see your sister Judy this trip. Don't forget to bring me a prayer-book for McDade."

It was a beautiful morning, that of their sailing. The quay was crowded with people laughing and weeping. The young were anxious to sail; the old full of fear and mistrust. Fair boys and rosy-faced girls were taking their last look of Ireland, which, never again to be seen, was to be until their dying day called by that delicious word, *home*. Yes, they would settle and build homes in other lands, marry and rear families, but the land of their birth was to be forever their first love. The gray Irish skies, the yellow corn, the green grass, the crystal rivers that had entranced their early life, kept, ever afterwards, its magic spell.

A voice, tremulous and sad, began in Gaelic a prayer. It was Malachy's. The crowd knelt on the shining sand-strip repeating responses. The voices of old bare-headed men and women, their white hair straggling in the crisp, light morning breeze, came charged with emotion loud and long; the voices of the younger came quick, were half-notes of sorrow and half of merriment. Golden youth will not be manacled by sorrow.

"Nelly," said a tottering old man to a beautiful girl that was clinging to him and kissing his wrinkled face, "mind your religion; be a good girl. God will take care of you. If you ever come back—I won't be here; but come to my grave and that of your mother, and pray for us. It's hard to part with you, Nelly, but the landlord has all, and the poorhouse will give me a sheltering."

"Good-by, Thady," said a weak-voiced old woman. "You're all I have, but it's better for ye to be goin' where you'll do well than starving here. Don't forget Mary."

Just then James Fortune, wondering why any one could sorrow at leaving Ireland for America, beheld on the edge of the strand a gray mare well known to him, and astride of her Egbert Brown, closely scrutinizing those going aboard. The gang-plank was taken in; the third whistle blown. The *Blackbird* turned seaward, and James Fortune, now safe, waved his hand to Mr. Brown, made faces gleefully, and bade garrets and Irish poorhouses farewell.

Pocket-handkerchiefs waved from the sea-going ship, and those on land heard the showman's voice singing in a broken way:

' Adieu to Ballyshannon, where I was bred and born!
Go where I may, I'll think of you, as sure as night and morn."

CHAPTER IX.

A MAN OF FORTUNE.

"THAT's the *Blackbird* just coming in," said a stout, ruddy-faced man standing on the pier. "She's in earlier than I had any mind of," he continued, pulling a large gold watch attached to a huge gold chain from his pocket. "And she looks as if she had been dancing the half of the way. I'll warrant that her cargo is glad to get ashore, and small blame to them. I have been there before and know a thing or two about the Blackbird."

The speaker was addressing three young women who were anxiously straining their eyes in the direction of the fast-approaching ship.

"True for you, Mr. McDade," said one of them, wiping away the tears that memory had brought. "We all know the *Blackbird*; we all have had a taste of her. She has left more in the deep than she brought ashore. I trust in God that my sister, Sally Kerrigan, is safe and sound. Oh, dear! I hope she is—I hope she is!"

"Never fear that," said Mr. McDade. "A Donegal woman is like a cat. She has nine lives. Where are you going to take her when she lands? If you have no place, leave her up at our house. You know anybody from Donegal has but to open my door and make themselves at home. There is always a bed and a bite for them."

"We know that, Jamie. You wouldn't be your father's son if there was anything stingy about you," spoke the three women as one.

"As to what I am going to do with my sister Sally," said the first woman speaker, "I have no great plans laid. I'll take her to myself up in the country, in Connecticut. Servants are scarce up there, and there's great asking for them and big pay. Sally won't find much trouble in getting a place. It's better for her to come with me than staying here. It's my opinion that too many of the Irish hang around New York."

"That's easy saying, Mary, and perhaps a bit true; but you must remember that the most of them land here without a penny in their pockets. Who's going to advance them any? Let us take the *Blackbird's* cargo," continued Mr. McDade. "How much money have they? and, more, they're not like the other people that comes here, for they have neither larning nor trades. You see there's two ways to wink at a thing. If they go to the country, what do they know about farming? So they sit themselves down here, and I don't much blame them.

Folks like to be where they get something to do."

"Well, Jamie, it's not everybody that gets on like you. If they all did, I would have nothing to say about their stopping."

"Mary, I had my knocks as well as the rest of them. It was not all pie with me."

"Whatever you have you deserve it," said the three women in chorus.

"Here she is!" said McDade. "Don't forget, girls, but come and see me, and bring your greenhorns along. I want to hear all about the old 'dart.' I live only a few blocks from here—just around the corner. I'll run and tell my folks that the *Blackbird's* in, so they'll have something hot ready."

Jamie McDade was soon lost around the corner.

"Hasn't he done well in this country!" said Mary Kerrigan. "Made a mint of money, I'm told; but he deserves it, so he does. His house and pocket are open to everybody from the North. His wife is not like him, and his child—mercy upon me! she has more airs than the landlords' children in Ireland. The Irish in this country spoil their children by letting them have too much of their own way. I met his daughter and she was mocking us all, speaking of greenhorns, and her father and mother once as green as the rest of us. On her account I don't like to go near the house. She had the impudence to tell me one day that one religion was as good as another. The brazen-faced thing! I could hardly keep my hands off her. If her grandfather heard such talk out of her head, he would pull her limb from limb. I suppose she'll be like some of the rest of the Irish—go over for style."

"There goes the gang-plank, Mary," said one of her companions. "Let us get near it, the way we will see every one coming off—the closer the better. Hurry up with ye! Don't you see the captain himself on the deck, and the passengers beginning to come? Hurry up, I tell ye!"

The girl was right. What a change had taken place on the long sea-voyage! Could Malachy McCrudden have seen his wan, emaciated countrymen and countrywomen leave the emigrant-ship, what would have been his thoughts? He would have looked in vain for many faces, laughing faces that had sailed from his little seaport town for the land of their dreams, the great America, but by adverse gales landed in a port whence no stranger returns.

A crowd of friends, weeks in waiting for the overdue emigrant-ship, hastily gathered on the pier to welcome their relatives, and to take them to resting-places.

Among the first to disembark was Sally Kerrigan, weeping with joy that she had escaped the power of the wild, foam-spitting sea. She was followed by the showman, pale, haggard, unsteady in his gait, carrying, or rather dragging, her rough black satchel containing the few belongings that were her fortune.

In a moment she was in the arms of her sister— the sister that had worked hard in the new land, and laughed at the toil, buoyed up by the hope that her earnings were to bring her brothers and sisters to the land of their dreams. Sal was the first, and Sal would help others to follow.

"Oh, Mary, I thought I should never see you again!" cried the excited girl. "Mary Hart and Jennie Farley, that came with me, died of the ship's fever. Oh! Mary, if their folks would know what they done to them, they would gather the whole country and murder Captain Campbell. I was there when they buried Mary Hart. They put her in a black canvas bag, with weights to her feet, and two sailors, one at the head—and you know what a fine head she had—the other at her feet, and they swung her into the ocean for the sharks. I shut my eyes, but the splash made me sick. Before that the captain said, 'Come, now, boys and girls, pray for your friend.' So while we were praying he was reading, with tears in his eyes, from a book. But I couldn't begin to tell you how many died. I would have died only for that young man," pointing to the showman, "and another one that hasn't come off yet."

"What's his name, Sal?" said Mary, eying curiously the sick stranger, "and where is he going?"

"His name is Rob McClintock, that's what it is, and where he's going he don't know, as he don't know a soul on this side of the sea—not a soul. He says if he gets work around, the first money will take him wherever we may be. It will be a kind of lonesome without him. When he's at himself, he can whirl like a hoop, caper like a monkey, and sing like a thrush. You cannot judge him now, for he has worn himself out attending all the girls aboard. My! I wish he was coming with us. I'm sure if you heard him sing, or saw him dance once, that would gain you right away."

"Well," said Mary, "introduce us and we'll bring him along. If he is all you say, whatever we lay out on him, he'll give it back."

"That he will, and more, for he's all heart," said the well-pleased Sal.

"We'll take care of him," said Mary's two friends, looking into their purses. "But, Sal, you have not told us anything about home."

"Wait until we get from here," said Mary.

"Then let us go at once," said the two friends.

"Come here, Rob," shouted Sal, "and shake hands with my sister Mary and her two friends—cousins of ours, the McCaffrey girls from our place. They are all going to take you along and show you a bit of the country. You said you wanted to be wherever I was, and now is your chance. I told them what a lot of things you could do."

"Let us go, Sal," said Mary. "Your other friend must have got off unknownst to us. It's not in Donegal you are now; you cannot find a body you're after so easy. He may be miles away. There are cars running everywhere in this country. You cannot tell where he has scooted to. Come, let us be making a start. I'll warrant you're as hungry as a hawk. Around the corner we'll get a bit."

The little band was on the point of moving away, when a rough-looking country boy joined them.

"That's the one! that's the one!" said Sal, twitching Mary's arm, "that's James Fortune! He's an orphan—a poorhouse boy that ran away. That's him. He was the only one on the ship that wasn't sick. He kept us alive with his ghost and fairy stories that he heard from the old paupers. Yes, that's him. Where are you going, Jamie? I'm going away—far away; and Rob is going; we are all going. Do you stop here?"

There were tears in the boy's eyes, quickly brushed away with his baggy sleeve, as he spoke:

"I don't know, Sal, where I am going. I have enough money to see me through a week. Malachy gave it to me, and he gave me also his sister Judy's address, but I lost it. I'll get a job. They say there's work here for everybody, and I'm thinking there is. I wish I was going with you. Wouldn't I like it! I'll miss Rob. Rob, you're great company. I was just thinking, as I got off that gang-plank, that old Brown and his crazy wife will have a long hunt for me. I am going to James McDade's. I hear he is a great man—very rich. The captain sends me with a prayer-book from Malachy. The captain says he took that way of getting me something to do. He might give me a job. I suppose I'll have to go."

There were handshakings, weepings, and promises, vows of remembrance; then the little band started for their Connecticut home, while James Fortune, wondering at everything his eyes saw, sped his way to the well-known café of James McDade.

By asking every few yards he found where McDade lived. He was soon in front of a large, brick building ornamented with a flaming yellow sign, telling to all who passed by the way that "Whiskies, Wines, Ales, and Beer" were constantly on hand and of the best quality. Men were passing out and in through the little wicker door. There was music, laughter, and loud talk.

James Fortune, gazing at the well-dressed men that passed him, and then looking at his own ill-shapen clothes, felt himself crushed with shame, and his feet unwilling to carry him further on his errand.

"Everybody is rich in this country," he was muttering to himself. "I don't wonder that people stand so much hardship to get here."

Just then a colored troop, preceded by a brass band, came down the street, followed by a jostling, whistling crowd.

A sight so strange, and a fear that they might make him a butt for their sport, drove him into the café. The place was filled with men, some telling stories, others in business conversation. He allowed his eyes to wander over the café and delight in its polished furniture and bevelled mirrors, its shelf after shelf of glittering glasses, its shining faucets and ornamented kegs, and the quickness and cleanliness of the three barkeepers in their immaculate white coats and aprons. At the end of the bar stood a pleasant-faced man, one hand in his trousers pocket, the other toying with his ponderous gold chain, his hat tilted back, carelessly surveying the place.

"That's one of the greenhorns just off the ship. Ain't he a sight! I wonder what tailor cuts his clothes—cuts in the new style, I'm thinking," laughingly spoke one of the bartenders.

These words brought a frown from the pleasant-faced man, who motioned to the object of the barkeeper's jest to approach him.

"I'm looking for James McDade," said the Irish lad. "Malachy McCrudden, of his place, sends him a prayer-book. I have it here."

"I am the man. And this book, you tell me, comes from Malachy? Dear old Malachy, it's worth ten times its size in gold to me!" There were tears in the speaker's eyes—tears begot by the memories of other days which flitted through his brain.

"Who are you anyway?" he continued. "Have you ever heard of Jimmie McDade that fought Wilson on the old Mall? I guess you have. For Malachy's sake you're as welcome here as one of my own. You don't look overcrowded with the world's gifts, but who does that leaves Ireland these times? Never mind; it won't be always that way. There's better times a-coming for the Old Land. Even if we have to leave her, we don't give her up by any means. If I had a son—I have only a daughter—I would train him up to strike a blow for the old dart. Donegal must be changed; I guess I would hardly know it, though I would wager that I'd find my way there yet. Many a pleasant day I had over there. Malachy could tell you many a yarn about me, that he could. Curse on the landlords that drove you and me out of it! Their day of reckoning will soon come. Just think! Lord Daffadowndilly's estate is the ancestral home of the McDades. You didn't know that, yet it's the fact. Instead of selling whiskey over a counter, I ought, if things had gone right, been an Irish gentleman following the hounds or something as easy. I wonder if the upstarts know that their end is so near. I'll bet they don't. It's just as well; they'll better be able to take their medicine. When I think of them I am sick. I lay in Lifford jail for six months because I tried to stop one of the young Daffadowndillys and his friends from riding through my father's best field of oats. We'll ride through their parks when we go over there, and we won't even as much as say 'by yer leave' for the liberty. It's a wonder that Malachy said nothing to you, seeing he had the tip; but maybe he thought you too young. However, you'll grow."

James Fortune soon told his story—a story that thoroughly pleased McDade, and drew from him such expressions as " Your a brick !" " A boy of your nerve will make out."

James McDade's imagination was lively. In the ill-clad, wondering boy that stood before him he beheld a persecuted child of his race, whose parents were undoubtedly evicted from their homes and, dying by the wayside, left their boy to be brought up in that ill-boding, detested place, an Irish poorhouse. His running away from the Browns, " miserable Cromwellian settlers," was an act of courage that showed the spirit of his race and demonstrated beyond cavil that the youth had a good drop in his veins. Such a boy, the bearer of his prayer-book, the friend of his friend Malachy McCrudden, should not be friendless and homeless in the great city while

James McDade had employment to give and a house over his head.

"You have no place to work, and I think you had better stay with me. You could clean up and do little jobs around until such times as we find you a better job. Rome wasn't built in a day. That's an old and true saying. Everybody must take his turn, and that means waiting. Do you know, I think it is a good thing, for when you wait for a thing, it's worth something when you get it. And now a word: Don't tell any mortal soul, after me, on your life, now, I warn you, anything about that poorhouse business. Keep that to yourself, as the less folks know about you in this country the better. The people that get along over here are the close-mouthed. If you tell your business to anybody here it will soon be everybody's business. What do you say about remaining with me?"

"I'll stay, Mr. McDade, and do everything—anything. I have no friends. I don't know anybody. I had one address, but I lost it. Malachy gave it to me, the address of his sister Judy. I suppose you know her. Captain Campbell said you knew everybody worth knowing, and if he wanted to meet anybody he went to your house."

"Your name is James Fortune. Well, James, the captain about hit it. I know pretty much of everybody that comes from around home. They make their headquarters here. Of course, I know Judy and her husband—one of the finest men that ever stepped in shoe-leather. Why shouldn't I know 'em? It was to their house I came when I first landed, and well they received me; besides I stood for her only child, little Genevieve, the most cunning little girl you ever met, as full of fun as an egg's full of meat. I have not seen them in a long time, more the shame for me to have to own it! But a man in my business must be always around. I never go home to dinner; my old friend Hoffman on the next block has a fine restaurant; we can eat there, and then go over to Seligman's, a Jew friend of mine, and he'll rig you out. A shave to take that down off you, a trimming of your locks, and a new suit will make a swell of you. It was John Swanton, Judy McCrudden's man, that bought me my first Yankee suit. Come! I guess you're hungry; they don't overfeed on the *Blackbird*."

As James McDade led the way, followed by his young protégé, one of the bartenders remarked to his fellows: "I'll bet a new hat that the greenhorn will have on a white apron and be back of this counter to-morrow. Mac will have him transformed into a dude before he presents him to Mrs. Mac. We're safe anyway, boys. Mac don't discharge. The more comes the merrier and the easier."

The bartender's prophecy came true. The next

morning, who could guess that the neatly—yea, more, flashily—clad boy was Jimmie Fortune, the runaway emigrant?

He was shown his place behind the huge bar, and in a few months' time had become an expert in sliding beer-mugs and mixing pleasant beverages. Every evening he was allowed to attend the district night-school. McDade was a power in his ward; he was a politician, but a politician of a strange sort—a politician without personal ambition. He was always at the beck of his friends with work, advice, and purse, but the trouble of office was too much for this easy-going Irishman.

James Fortune listened with open-mouthed wonderment to McDade's tales of "put-up jobs," "deals," bribes whereby the party in power kept itself there.

None of these tales, nor the lessons drawn from them, were lost on the ambitious youth, who could not understand how a man of McDade's seeming ability allowed his friends to pay him in easy-mouthed praise while retiring with the spoils.

At the age of twenty-two a chance gave James Fortune what McDade rightly called "the hoist of his life." There had been a mighty war in the district between Tom Gilligan and Mike Clancy for the honor of representing the district in Congress. Halls had been hired by both candidates and meetings held nightly, each candidate denouncing his rival with all the power of speech and imagination he could muster. Their friends were busy in canvassing, betting, and holding pyrotechnic displays. Bands nightly paraded the streets, carrying transparencies which told of the virtues of their friend, the vices of their obstinate foe, who was already " licked out of his boots."

The night before election was announced to be the " grand rally," when all the friends were " to put in an appearance." Eminent speakers were to address the meeting. The Hon. Jacob Schneider, of Yonkers; the Hon. Patrick O'Toole, Hoboken; the Hon. Isaac Levy, Staten Island; Aldermen Gruber, Barzinski, etc., etc., so the large posters announced, were to be on hand to tell the people why their candidate should be elected.

Clancy's candidature was the least inviting. Yet it had been espoused with all the enthusiasm of McDade's ardent nature.

"For the first time in your life, Mac, you'll be beaten hands down. You'll have to swallow Gilligan whole," was the shout of the Gilligan crowd as they passed the Irishman's business place.

"Not if I know myself, boys. Too early to tell what's coming out of the set-eggs," was his reply, as he laughingly stood by the side of the little wicker door.

It was not McDade's way to hurry, but those in his

store the night of the "grand rally" saw him running around, whispering to this and that partisan, a look of despair on his face. When a telegraph-boy gave him a despatch he hurriedly adjusted his eye-glasses, read the despatch, wrung his hands, stamped his feet, and muttered through his clenched teeth what some said was a curse, others a threat.

"I knew it! Yes, I did! He's a traitor, and I'll get even with him if it takes me forty years. The other side have got him. I always had my doubts of his backbone; now it's all cleared up. He's a coward, and a cutthroat at that, he is!" exclaimed the furious McDade.

"What is it all about?" queried the guests, gathering in a circle around the landlord.

"I never saw you so mad before in all my life, Mac; you would think that it was after election, and our friend Clancy defeated," said one of the circle.

This sally brought laughter and had the effect of restoring McDade to his easy-going and natural way.

"You would be mad, too, if you depended on a man—just as sure of him as sure could be—and when it comes to the eleventh hour he coolly gets sick and, informing you of the fact, leaves you in the lurch. Now," continued McDade, "I would rather die than do a trick like that. Why don't he come out like a man, and say plump, 'I have changed my mind and gone over to the Gilligans'? But no; he shouts Clancy, and Clancy, until the times comes for him to throw off his coat and get to work; then he gets sick, and here we are in a mess! I'll read the telegram, and then you'll know it all as well as myself. The whole thing through is an infernal piece of scoundrelism, and that's my opinion. Listen, boys:

"'Regrets. Can't come. Down with pneumonia. Doctor says can't get out for weeks. I wish I could be with you to-night in the last skirmish, to rouse the boys for Clancy. But I will not be missed. Better men will fill my place. If I can't fight, I can pray for Clancy's victory.

"'JAMES HUNTER.'

"What do you think of that? He may keep his prayers. They would do us more harm than good. We don't want any hypocrite's prayers. We'll have to do the best we can without him, and we had better be going to the hall."

There was silence and well-evidenced gloom on the reading of Hunter's telegram. Mr. Hunter had a great reputation as a political speaker. He was quick to see an opponent's weak point, and happy in setting it forth in the worst light. He was never dry nor tiresome, taking care to sprinkle his discourse with funny sayings and well-told stories. He had studied and knew the crowd—felt their pulse in a moment, saw their hearts in their eyes, formed plans to capture them, and was generally successful. He was a practical politician, holding that "to the victor belongs the spoils," "in war everything is fair," and "leave your friend if you find a better." Reformers branded these sayings as base, but Mr. Hunter would tell the reformers that out of office they might hold to other maxims; in office they hugged and practised these same despised sayings. When such a man deserted, it was, argued the wise ones, for the same reason that a rat deserts a ship.

"It is too late now to get any one of any account to take his place," said one of the district leaders. "Let us go on with the meeting. The only way I see out of it is for you, Mac, to give us something yourself. No apologies, Mac; a few hot Scotches will give you the spirit. No man, I'll bet, will be better listened to. Come, now, Mac, and give us a lift."

"I couldn't get up and speak in front of a crowd if you made me mayor of New York! I'm not built that way. I haven't the training nor the education. I'm only for rough work."

"Why not give Fortune a chance?" suggested one of the bartenders. "He's always spouting around here. I have often heard him say that he could do as well as half the fellows he heard shooting off on platforms. It would do no harm to give him a chance. If he can't help, sure he can't hurt. One thing I can tell you, boys, he won't falter for want of gab. If you want him, as soon as he comes from his supper I'll send him down to the hall; that is, if you say so."

"Well, just as John says, he can't hurt us a bit—that's sure; so why not give the youngster a chance? If you don't try these young fellows you will never know what's in them. I vouch that he won't break down; he's not of the soft brand. Let him take my place. What's your opinion?"

There was a hearty *yes* to McDade's question, and the bartender was told to hunt up James Fortune.

Concordia Hall was filled to overflowing with followers of both candidates. They had come to hear the Hon. James Hunter, to enjoy his latest witty sayings. They had heard the other speakers and were growing tired and impatient. Some were leaving the hall. At this juncture Mr. McDade shouted: "Fortune! Fortune!" The crowd took up the shout and yelled itself hoarse, and kept on yelling until a handsome, finely dressed young man at the rear end of the platform arose, advanced towards his audience, and began talking with the utmost confidence and coolness, silencing the audience in a moment. As he warmed up in his speech he became fiery and cutting. He painted Clancy as a man born on Irish soil, bred in the fairest land the sun shines upon, loving that land, becoming a member of a society vowed to free that land, and banished—his only crime. He would not sell that land. The leaving his native land, the cruel partings, the voyage on the fever-ships, the landing and the rise of Clancy from a 'longshoreman, his simplicity that no honors could destroy, his generosity—all were held up to the audience with a fire and earnestness that spell-bound them.

"You should vote for Clancy," said the young orator, " because Clancy is an exile from his country, and for a reason that does honor to the man. He loved Ireland and he hated England. Will you, exiles of Erin, blame Clancy for following not only in your footsteps, but in those of every Irishman who is not a craven or a coward ? Clancy is proud of being an Irishman; he does not deny it. He has not changed his name, nor vowed that his ancestors came over in the *Mayflower*. He admits that he is Irish, and Irish to the backbone. I have heard them say, these Yankees, on the streets that they will vote for Gilligan, because Gilligan, at any rate, was born over here, while Clancy is but a greenhorn. They think they could make a tool of Gilligan; they know that they can never touch Clancy. Irishmen ! exiles ! what answer will you give these politicians who loathe you because you are Irish ? I know an answer that will humble them in the dust. I hold in my hand here a telegram from the Hon. James Hunter to the friend of all of you, honest James McDade. Hunter says he is sick, and he says it at the eleventh hour; but it's not the first time the Irish made the Sassenach sick. We can do without him. We will thank him for his kindness by voting for Clancy."

As Fortune finished his audience went wild, shouting for Clancy and booing for Hunter and everything he was supposed to represent. On all sides it was said that young Fortune was a coming man, a saying emphasized the next morning with half a column in *The Morning Democrat*.

"The unexpected is always happening," said Disraeli. It is an aphorism that one may hold with no little security. Gilligan and his friends were so confident of success that they had ordered a banquet to celebrate the victory. They had also, as they boldly avowed, steeped a rod in vinegar for McDade. When, then, contrary to all expectation, the news came that Clancy was elected by a large majority, the word sped rapidly through the district that young Fortune and his speech were the making of the Hon. Mike Clancy. From that moment he was no longer the obscure bartender of James McDade, but a man of "pull" and power. Clancy was of that type of politicians who hold that a friend in need is a friend indeed, and at any rate he had learned that young Fortune could be·a dangerous enemy. It was but the work of a wise man to bind him to his standard.

The Hon. Mike Clancy was a cellar-digger : few things in those days paid better. His triumphant election meant more contracts than he could well fulfil; besides most of his time would now be spent in making laws. Supervision by some one interested in his business was necessary. After a talk with McDade the firm of Clancy & Fortune was founded. At the suggestion of the junior member the firm branched out in various directions. James Fortune, who had won his hold by politics, had no intention of abandoning that which so speedily put him on the road to success. He founded the "Shamrock Club," which met weekly at McDade's to discuss the best means of freeing Ireland—and at the same time of holding a grip on New York. This club in a few months became so large that a hall was rented, and despite the protests of James Fortune, their president, who wished to call the hall "The Sarsfield," was named Fortune Hall. The president graciously submitted, claiming as his privilege the right to decorate the interior in a suitable manner, which was done to their taste. The decorations consisted of green flags, green ribbons, framed pictures of Saint Patrick banishing snakes, Brian Boru in his tent, Sarsfield in battle array, Emmet in a reverie, O'Connell on Tara's hill, framed sentiments, mostly warnings to "cruel England," that the day of retribution was near at hand, and if she valued her safety she would relax her grip on green Erin.

At the end of the hall was a streamer on which was sewed in large golden letters: " We Come From The Thirty-two Counties Of Ireland! We Are The Kindly Irish!"

About this time the death of Peter Quigley made a vacancy in the board of aldermen, and the news being discussed at the Shamrock Club, one of the members, pointing to the motto on the streamer, said: " Let us show how kindly we can be by electing our president in Quigley's place. I don't want to say much against the dead—I guess they had better rest —but you all know what I'm going to say just as well as I do, that Quigley, before he got office, talked nothing but 'Ireland, Ireland,' and what he would do for the Irish, but as soon as he had his fat job he forgot all his promises, and he and his family became so proud that they would as lief meet the devil as one of us. I tell you, he is not the first that has risen through us, and, when up, despised us, and forgot the shoulders on which he mounted. What do you think, boys, of my suggestion? It's as good as they make them."

That evening a committee waited on James Fortune, tendered him the nomination and their support, which was later ratified by the regular organization, making, as it did, the best of a bad matter. To oppose the Shamrock Club would have been poor and foolish policy, and from politics we expect the wisdom found in the vulgar phrase, "Save your own bacon every time."

A few weeks later Alderman Fortune, fresh from his glory, at the age of twenty-eight, and much to the mind of Mrs. McDade, whose ideas were high and whose mourning was constant over what she called "the slackness of her husband for honors," called at the McDade residence on a pleasant errand. He was met by Mrs. McDade, a short, stout woman, resplendently clad.

He was led into the spacious parlor and seated himself at the wave of her bejewelled hand.

Mrs. McDade, in her own way, was gracious and talkative, and the alderman was full of pleasantry.

"I knew you would be elected," said Mrs. McDade. "I told the governor so. How your people, if they were alive, would rejoice! Mr. Mac told me that your family was one of the best, if not the very best, in the county he comes from, but that they sacrificed all for Ireland. That Irish business is wearying, but you dare not say a word about it when the governor is around. I see he has you in it. You are a young man, and, if you take a woman's advice, you will leave the Irish severely alone. Mr. Mac makes his living out of them, but you're now where you can afford to ignore them, and you can do it easily; besides you have such a name that nobody would put an Irish construction upon it. What can you make out of McDade, even if the governor wanted to give it a twist? No matter how you roll it, 'tis Irish and nothing else. Of course, if the governor was around I would lose my head for less than I've said to you. You know he lives on his imagination. According to his story, he will free Ireland, and then he and I and Miss Molly, so he says, will own Daffadowndilly Castle and have nothing to do but give orders and have them obeyed. I tell him that he had better attend to his business and leave the Daffadowndillys alone, for if they ever catch him over there they'll give him a life-sentence.

"Then it is enough to drive me wild, the kind of characters he's in with in this Irish business—hod-carriers, carpenters, bricklayers, and that set, with their thick tongues, and their thick brogans, wandering over the brussels, and in danger of breaking my brickety-back. Poor Molly, she dare not say 'boo.' No; the governor will have nothing here but Irish, and so I and his poor girl must suffer. The other night the poor, dear child went with the Flammers to the Episcopals, and maybe she will never hear the last of that! The governor was like a wild man; cried like a child, said it was the first disgrace in his family, and if she ever went there again she should never darken his door. When the row was over I stole into her bedroom and told her to go when she felt like it, and not mind her father's bad tongue. I suppose she won't be long with us. Mr. Mac told me to-day at dinner that you were coming to-night to see me on a little business. I can easily guess what it is. Molly herself has given me an inkling of it. Well, when I married McDade I took my own advice and pleased myself, so it's for Molly to do the same. She has taken a fancy to you, and I will not, indeed, gainsay it. If she burns her fingers she cannot blame me. Molly is the finest girl in the city, the only thing we have to make us happy, and whoever gets her will have to live with us for a spell. We couldn't see her leaving us."

Mrs. McDade sobbed violently, and Miss Molly, hearing her mother, was soon by her side.

The lovers had long agreed. The consent of the mother, now given, was all that was needed.

The day after the marriage the generous McDade presented his daughter a fine residence, boasting, as he signed the transfer papers, that the first male of the line of Fortune and McDade should have a similar present.

This honestly meant boast was never to be put into effect. It was a spiritual writer with much foresight who said that in the midst of life we are in death. Happy in his daughter's marriage and in his new son's schemes and speculations, McDade planned away into the future, promising himself in the not distant time that sweetest of pleasures, children's loving prattle.

Merry are the bird-songs in the crisp spring morn, merry are the voices of the loitering brooks, but merrier far the babbling speech from children whose chubby little hands toy with your face, whose laughing little eyes tell the old, old story of love!

A cold, laughed at at first, then doctored, off and on, at the request of friends, finally settled into pneumonia. Medical skill was useless. The big, brave, generous Irishman, who had watched so many ships come into port, who had welcomed so many immigrants to his home and helped them with his purse, lay cold and dead in the handsome house where he had dreamed of romping with his grandchildren.

It is said that the dreams of our early life press upon us closer as death comes. "Poor Mac," as they called him—those who made his district, and they were of every nationality—in his last illness sang of his native Donegal, wept for his Erin, gave the command to his soldiers to charge Daffadowndilly Castle and hoist the standard of the dauntless McDades. A few minutes before he died, the battle was over. He had conquered; the Daffadowndillys were in flight; he was lord and master of his ancestral estates; the dream of his life had been fulfilled. Those who surrounded his bedside heard him say, as a momentary consciousness came to him: "Read over me from Malachy McCrudden's prayer-book." But that gleam of reason faded, and as lord and chief of his clan, in full possession of his dream, passed away what bluff old Captain Campbell, with honest tears in his eyes, called "the tenderest heart that I ever brought over the sea."

At his death his property passed into the hands of James Fortune, whose business capacity and power of amassing wealth were well understood.

It was the opinion of those who were keen judges that the income of the property would increase in the new hands, and the thought was right as evidenced in the succeeding years.

With Fortune as alderman and Clancy in Congress, the contracts for work grew yearly, until ten years after the company's inception its founders were reckoned worth a quarter of a million dollars each. It was then that Clancy sold out his interest to his partner, resigned his seat in Congress, and withdrew to spend the remainder of his life in his fine country mansion at New Rochelle. Before he resigned he so arranged it that his old business associate found no difficulty in occupying his long-coveted seat in Congress.

This new honor brought the Fortunes to Washington, and with them came the jubilant mother-in-law, now Mrs. Dade. She was filled with the ambition to dazzle, and her word in the household was law. Daily in her barouche the young Fortunes, gayly dressed, clustered around her. She drove on Pennsylvania Avenue, her quick eyes seeing the latest fads of fashion, and noting them for consultation with her daughter. The fourth child, Chichester Hartley Fortune, was born in Washington, and at the request of the Chichesters, for whom it was named, was baptized in St. John's Episcopal Church, one of the presents on this occasion coming from the President, with a little note which Mrs. Dade treasured to her dying day and showed to all her friends as evidence of the high standing of the Fortunes. When Mr. Fortune's time in Congress expired he returned to New York and purchased the Wormley residence on Fifth Avenue, from which date his former political friends noted a change. At the request of Mrs. Dade, but very willingly complied with, the Hon. Mr. Fortune resigned the presidency of the Shamrock Club, and sent brief letters of resignation to the various Irish organizations to which he belonged and through which he had received his rise and fortune. When these notes were read, they brought to his associates the old story of the result of mounting a beggar on horseback. There were two listeners who had other thoughts—the bartender who first launched him into political life and the man who first pressed his name as the genuine Irishman who should take Quigley's place. One said to himself: " This patriotism is a humbug, and the quicker we learn that those professing Irish patriots are in the thing for a living the better." The other: " Whom can you trust these days? It was Father James Cahill that knew them when he said: ' John, have nothing to do with them. I am thirty-two years as a priest in New York, and have some experience, and in all that time I have not met one of those political chaps who talked Ireland, and, thanks to the foolish Irish, rose to big positions, who did not, as soon as his purse was fat enough, turn on them, insult them, and know them no more; keep away from them, John.' I wished I had taken his advice, but it's not too late yet to warn my children. This is only the beginning. We won't have long to wait for the end."

" Coming events," sang the poet, " cast their shadows before," and the burden of his song was right.

To an invitation of the Shamrock Club to dine with them on St. Patrick's Day and respond to the toast " The Irish in America," the Hon. James Fortune sent a curt note stating that he no longer believed in fostering the spirit of nationality in free America—that there should be neither Irish, French, nor German in America, but Americans; and that those who did not like to be Americans should go where they could be Irish, French, or German.

The reading of this note brought curses and threats, but there were those of the club who were sad and silent, blaming themselves for putting him into a position to ignore their threats and curses, and through that position to amass enough wealth to make the position secure.

At the St. Andrew's Society dinner, which Mr. Fortune later attended, he boasted of his ancestors, strong of limb and sparing of speech, who had come to Ireland from that land of lands, the home of Walter Scott and Bobby Burns. He was proud of being Scotch-Irish, and with pride he referred to what those of that race had done in the upbuilding of the great American people. Some of them, he continued, had like himself been born in Ireland—a mere accident; but their love of Scotland was, if he might say so, strengthened instead of weakened by that accident.

One part of his speech was loudly applauded:

"Gentlemen, while I pride myself in being a scion of that wonderful race, the Scotch-Irish, and while I pride myself on the battles of my ancestors for holding aloft the banner of Presbyterianism amid a hostile race, I at the same time put my Americanism above all things. I hold that America is the greatest land under high heaven, and to be a citizen of this land is the highest honor a mortal can enjoy. It behooves us who are here to-night to vow that this land shall never become the prey of any potentate whatsoever, temporal or spiritual, king or pontiff. It behooves us to maintain, even with our lives, the little red schoolhouse which has done so much for the commonwealth; it behooves us to keep the State and Church apart, and to blend all people into the American people—a people destined to be the liberators of humanity!"

This speech as reported in the morning journals was the last straw to break the camel's back. It severed the last tie with his old friends. Even Clancy, a few weeks after, shut the door in his face and spoke of him as a renegade and a scoundrel.

The loss of these old associates worried not the Hon. James Fortune. New associates of high standing, as the world counts, were at his beck. Mrs. Dade was glad that her distinguished son-in-law had cut loose from the "low Irish," and was with his family hereafter to be in the ranks of the swell set and best blood. Fortune was his name, and verily the Fortunes were in the swim.

CHAPTER X.

THE VOICE OF THE CHARMER.

The morning was a threatening gray, spurting now and then a few large drops of rain, just like a baffled child knowing not whether to laugh or cry. A mass of sunshine lit up for a moment the rain-touched leaves, a robin as if inspired dashed out a throatful of music, and down came the white rain, heralded by a low, laughing thunder-boom over the hills. The dry July dust, sport of the lightest breeze, blinding to the eyes, became a foot-paste. The cry once over, the sun came forth, scattering the clouds and bathing the entire valley in sunshine.

Père Monnier's eyes gazed with delight around him, quick to catch the ever-varying scenes of a summer's morning in his Adirondacks.

"That bit of rain was healthy and cooling, Père," said Napoleon in passing. "It settled the dust and gives a new color to the grass. It was badly needed, as everything was parched and dry as kindling-wood. You'll see a big crowd here to-day; a big crowd, I'm saying, for the rain is all over, and folks won't be afraid to get out. If it went on spitting now and then, as it did last year at this time, why there would be no use in making preparations; but it's over for the day and we may go ahead and get the tables ready."

Napoleon sauntered to the large hall, which the Père had built when he first came among his people. This hall was erected over the horse-sheds—a plan that brought honor to what was considered the daring genius of Père Monnier. It was well and solidly built, commodious in every way. Here was the library,—for the Père held that no parish was thriving that lacked a library.

"Books," he used to say, "melt the winter away." And again, "If you have Dickens and Scott to sit by your fireside and tell their tales, you won't find the winter half so dreary. What makes time long is doing nothing."

His own purse and the love of his parishioners had filled the bookcase with more than two hundred volumes of stories written by men and women who told stories for the love of telling them. Books with panaceas for ills and messages to men had no place on these rough shelves. Dictionaries are scarce in the homes of the poor, who read not for knowledge but for amusement. On Sunday mornings the hall was used as a meeting-place before Mass, where the crops, the price of logs, the latest news in politics, might be discussed through clouds of strong-smelling tobacco-smoke.

Once a year this hall was used for a picnic, to which came all the parish, young and old. It was one of the great events, if not the greatest event, of the year. It was fittingly to prepare for it that Napoleon was so busily engaged in superintending the placing of tables, and giving them a suitable decoration for so merry a day. For this purpose the married ladies had come early, bringing with them their best potted plants and the freshest flowers of their gardens. As Napoleon was a man of travel, his taste directed all decorations. Plants and flowers were placed at his disposal. No hints would be tolerated by this travelled master. When Mrs. Thebaud thought to puzzle him by showing him a red hibiscus and asking him if, in the course of his travels, he had seen anything like that, he dumbfounded her by coolly replying: " In one of the countries that I was soldiering in, it was a very troublesome weed, as bad as the thistle up here."

Mrs. Thebaud, a motherly old soul, was indignant and would have appealed to Père Monnier, but the other women readily replied that great as was Père Monnier's knowledge of books, it was no greater than Napoleon's knowledge of dogs and flowers.

When the decorations were completed and the tables set for the dinner, Napoleon, full of pride in his handiwork, stole over to the house to invite Genevieve to come and express her admiration at his skill.

"Eh, Genevieve, you're a young lady now, and I want to give you a lesson how to decorate your own home when you have one; that is, after the Père and me and Anna die," said Napoleon, leading the way.

"The hall just looks fine. I'll bet it will please the Père. All the flowers in the parish were brought here for me to pick from, and do you know what I did first? I picked the best, quite a lot, too, for my girl. Oh, she's as handsome as a picture; not the kind of pictures around here, but the kind I saw when I was soldiering. I can tell you a lot about her, too, and you won't know her. Just listen: gold hair, as fine as silk and as light as a spider's web; a head like the statue men stand before and say nothing, that I saw when I was in Rome; eyes that shoot you and make you love dying. But I won't tell you any more, for fear you might know her and give her no peace to-day, and you know that wouldn't do."

"I give up the guess," said Genevieve, putting her arms around Napoleon's neck, "and I'll hold you here until you tell me who is your girl. I used to be your girl, but you're like all the men, changeable. It takes a woman to be constant. You know the poet says that men are deceivers. But tell me the name of your girl and I'll let you go."

"That is a secret, Genevieve, that cannot be broken by the mouth. But if you let me go, I'll give you the secret in another way. The young lady on whose breast you see me pin the roses, that will be my girl; no mistake about it."

As soon as Napoleon was released, he hurried to a cupboard in the hall and brought from it the fairest flowers of the parish, and deftly selecting the comeliest, hurried back to Genevieve and pinned the beautiful bouquet on her breast.

"I know who is your girl now," sang Genevieve. "I knew it all the time, but I was just having fun with you. I'm your girl, and, according to your description, a pretty one. The flowers will make me prettier."

"Now, my little V., when we look at a statue, we don't think of the decorations."

"Napoleon! you know Anna calls you a flatterer."

"Anna has never travelled, my dear; her criticism doesn't count."

"What are you going to do with the other flowers in the cupboard, Napoleon?"

"Give them to my girl, of course, to decorate Père Monnier's writing-desk. We must never forget the Père, no matter what fun is up. If anything happens to him, Genevieve, it will be a sad day for all of us. A month ago, says the Père to me: 'Napoleon, what are you thinking about ? I see you're in a brown-study. I suppose you're fighting over the old wars ?' 'Well, no, I'm not, either,' says I, 'though I often do that, too. I'm just thinking if there is any truth in the yarn Billy Buttons tells of the fish that can be caught by the new-fangled kind of rod that a "sport" gave him. If there is, I would mortally like to have one of them same rods. I'm thinking I would have fish once in a while.' 'Well, Napoleon,' says he, 'that may come to you, if there is any truth in the old saying about all things coming to him who waits,' and off he went, as I thought for his mail, when, lo and behold you! what did he do but go and ask Buttons where a rod like his could be had, as Napoleon was hot after one of these same rods, and he would like to make me happy! 'Père,' said Buttons, 'I don't care for the rod. That is nothing against it, for it is the best rod I have ever handled; but since I had it I was just keeping a-thinking if it wouldn't suit Napoleon to a T. So, says I to myself, I'll give it to the Père as a present, to do what he likes with; but it would better please me if it went to Napoleon,' and no sooner said than he handed the rod to the Père. If Buttons gives a thing you must make no excuses, because there is no hypocrisy in Billy; what he offers is because he wants you to have it. So the Père brings along the rod without Anna or you or me seeing him, and puts it in my room with a piece of paper stuck around the butt. I opened it, and there was a picture of the Père giving me a rod. I was smiling all over me. Then he put in French, right at my foot, that the rod was given to Mr. Napoleon, the greatest of fishermen, in the hope that the table of Père Monnier would be well supplied with trout. Do you think I could ever forget that? Not I. I never forget a kindness. That makes me think of what Anna told me, that Ruth was married to a Mr. O'Connor. I wonder if he is rich and good-looking—things that count in a match these days. Ruth deserved a good man. I knew when she went away that she would not come back soon. But here are the folks a-coming, and I have not a drop of lemonade ready. Some folks can make people talk too much."

Napoleon was right. The folks were coming in all kinds of rigs—new, borrowed, and mended—loaded down with aprons of biscuits, each family vying to provide the best, large pans of baked beans, paper sacks of beef and pork, pies, and all the kinds of cake that are known to the Northland. There was pride pictured in every matron's face as she held the good things on her knee, her eyes looking to the parsonage for the familiar sight of Père Monnier and the shake of his hand, which more than repaid them for their days of cooking. The old had come to enjoy themselves as well as the young, and the enjoyments were many and within the reach of every pocket. The offices were various and well filled. Billy Buttons had a "throwing stand," consisting of three wires running parallel to each other, upon which were strung puppets. For five cents, the purchaser, standing at a measured distance, was allowed to throw five balls, while Buttons sang, "Hit a baby, take a cigar; no baby, no cigar." Napoleon, in the attitude of attention, and with a military sweep of his ladle, presided over the large tub of lemonade. Jim Weeks, as the proprietor of the only hotel in town, was deemed the proper man to sell the soft drinks. The best girl in the catechism class had the mighty privilege of selling the candies and nibbling them at her leisure. Her booth was the only one allowed in the hall, and the only one decorated. The other booths had places on the lawn. They were roughly constructed—a few barrels supporting planks—but "just the thing," said Weeks, "for people that came to enjoy themselves without airs or nonsense."

"Open that gate, man! open that gate and let us in. You'd think you were soldiering again and holding the fort. Don't be so slow, or we'll court-martial you!" spoke James Weeks as he banged, with his huge fists, at the gate that guarded the entrance to the hall. At the well-known voice, Napoleon rushed to the gate, put his key in the padlock, gave it a turn, and the entrance was clear, the picnic opened. The matrons hurried to deposit their baskets, parcels, and pans of good things in the little kitchen that was made in the loft of the hall. The men, after putting up their horses in the sheds, lit their pipes and strolled over the lawn, admiring the cunning ways in which Père Monnier had blended his flowers. Youngsters were cautioned not to touch a flower, as Napoleon had trained the big St. Bernard that lazily lay in passive dignity on the church step to swallow the first child that disturbed the plants.

There was a great shout, and it was to greet Père Monnier, who had just returned from a sick call, and was now sure to be in time for the dinner, the failure of which would have cast gloom on his people.

"Just in time, uncle! Just in time! The people were all afraid you could not get here, and Napoleon, as usual, was praying all kinds of prayers on folks that are mean enough to get sick on the one day in the year that they should keep well. You do not say what you think of your girl in the new dress you brought from Montreal."

"Bless my soul, Genevieve! I was just thinking that you are a little girl no longer, but a young lady, a big young lady! These roses are for me? My good girl, Genevieve, always thinking of me! I trust you always will. The house would be lonesome indeed without our girl."

"O uncle, you know I must always be your little

girl. If you should get angry with me, I should die. Don't I do everything I can to please you? And when you get the typewriter I will copy all your sermons and letters, and all you want me to do. I am your Genevieve."

"You are a good child, Genevieve; a very good child, dear; as thoughtful as if you were twice as old—a very good child, dear, and God send you to grow better and better. It is not enough to be good. We must keep on growing better. You remember the tableau that you were in: 'They who battle unto the end win the crown.'"

"Yes, that was pretty, uncle, but May Langtry nearly spoiled it when she ran off the stage," said Genevieve, running the paper-knife through Père Monnier's letters.

"A part is allotted to every one, Genevieve, and it must be rightly played," said the Père, while a serious mood stole over his pleasant face.

"You seem a little sad, uncle. Are you tired? Would you like to wash and rest a while before dinner? Perhaps dinner will not be in time, as the shower kept some of them late."

"Yes, dear, I feel a bit sad. When I went on the call a few hours ago, I thought I was to see old Bergeron, who is more than eighty, like a last leaf on a tree, ready to go at any time, cheerful old soul! but I was mistaken. It was to see his granddaughter, who married down East a worthless fellow, who soon got tired of her, trumped up charges against her, had one of these vile lawyers procure him a Western divorce, and now is married to some poor girl whose fate is soon coming. What puzzles most those who have not studied that most difficult of subjects, humanity, is that she still loves the rascal who has brought about her ruin, and tries to think that he could not be so base as to speak ill of her, whose love for him ate her up. This thought is but momentary, for then comes the reality. She is on her dying bed, poor little waif! and I must see her often and hold up to her the love of the Master, strong enough to cure all ills. I have been many years by sick-beds, but I have never been able to learn that callousness of death which doctors and some of my profession profess, by long experience, to attain. The story of this dying girl has made me weep big, salty tears; that it has, Genevieve! To-day the parish enjoys itself and doesn't think much of this poor creature, yet she once was 'the candy-girl.' 'Père,' said she, when I was leaving, 'I wish you would bring me a stick of candy from the booth, if for nothing else but to see it. You remember I was once your candy-girl, and see where I am now! O Père! I wish I was like that day. You must come and see me often. Do come and speak to me as you used to when I was in your catechism class. I will be your obedient little girl. I have done wrong in not listening to those whose advice was for my good, but I have suffered—suffered! and to whom can I turn if Père Monnier puts me away?' I thank God that you, Genevieve, are so sensible. Poor girl! Of course I will see her daily; and couldn't you study the cook-book for something light—very light—for her? You might, to-morrow, go with Napoleon and make a call. Sit by her bedside, show her by your eyes that you come not on any formal call, but rather as a sister, who would help her to battle for the crown. You cannot take her sufferings, dear—that is beyond us—but you can help her to conquer. It is love that this girl wants. She has seen so little of it that she partly doubts; but we must show her the error, and teach her to prepare for that coming love which is beyond all other love—the love of Christ.

"Yes, Genevieve; you are handsome, child. Tell Anna I said so. Run and get Anna, and we will all have dinner in the hall. I see Napoleon coming. Catch an old soldier not on the minute. There goes the bell!"

At the first note of the Angelus there was a holy silence, an uncovering and bending of heads, and a murmur of prayer. Old and young in reverent worship stood, until the old soldier dropped the bell-rope from his hand. Then there was noise and a rush, and a struggle for the dining-hall.

One table was kept for the Père; the others were free to all: first come first served was the understanding.

As soon as Père Monnier entered and said grace, there was a merry charge on the tables, a welcome ring of knives and forks, and that peculiar hum which comes from those who are well served, "the chuckling grunt human," as it has been called

Old Anna's eyes gazed long at the decorations, but when Napoleon suggested that she might learn a few points from his art, her eyes quickly rested on her plate and a look of contempt came to her features. She would not flatter one whom she believed could live on that airy kind of food.

"I have seen better in my day over in Canada, where the like of you thinks we have nothing, and then they were thought to be no great things," was Anna's stern reply to Napoleon's suggestions.

"I wonder," Anna continued, "that a man like you, who pretends to have been everywhere, though I'm not saying, mind ye, that you have been, couldn't bring back a little of it in your head. Your talk's your fortune, Napoleon. If you could only rein your tongue, everybody in the hall will hear your clatter before you're done. I don't see how the Père can sit up there and let you run on like a machine. Can't you let some one who has a check on himself speak? Listening, according to your count, is the only thing that you hadn't a rap at. Better try it, it's soothing; aye, soothing, Napoleon."

"Just hear her, Père," said Napoleon, with a look of intense disgust on his face, "bringing Canada into her talk, and saying she saw decorations like these there. Fie for shame, Anna! you have never travelled. I learned this mode of decoration from Signor Piombino, gardener in extraordinary to His Holiness. I say, Anna, do you hear that now?—gardener to His Holiness. Canada beats the Pope—it does, eh? Well, I guess not, and Père Monnier can't side with you on that point. Signor Piombino—mind the name, Anna—gardener to His Holiness."

"You're putting things in my mouth," said Anna hotly, "Mr. Napoleon, that I won't be after saying for you or any other body. I have as warm a wish for the Pope as you, and you're not going to bring me to any discussion with him. Clatter away now; I'm going to finish my dinner, that I be."

"Yes, let the discussion go for some other time," said the Père; "let us talk of something we can agree upon; Genevieve, for instance. I was just telling her how she has grown and how well she looks."

"See Anna's eyes now, Père," said Napoleon; "you have struck the right chord. Genevieve is Anna's decoration. She has fussed over her for days, ironing all the frills in the dress half a dozen times over and spending all morning plaiting her hair. As soon as I saw Genevieve I praised Anna's work. I am not jealous like some people I know; I have travelled. Show me a bit of art and I will admire without wanting to know who was the artist."

Anna was not to be provoked into speech by Napoleon's allusions, and Père Monnier, seeing that the old soldier was bent on making her lose patience, told a wonderful story of a dog, which at once turned the conversation for the remainder of the dinner-hour into the hands of the well-pleased Napoleon. Even Anna had to confess that the cause of much of her annoyance, talk on wars, dogs, and hunting, was vastly entertaining.

Dinner over, the tables were quickly cleared and removed while the chairs were packed in a corner, and word went forth that it was time to prepare for the dance. A little slim man, full of movement, drew his fiddle lovingly from a green bag and jumped on the platform, a seat of honor having been prepared for his coming. He was followed by smiling Frank Picquet, the best "caller" in the county. Soon the fiddle was in tune, partners ready—they had long been selected—and the order for "Moneymusk" was given. Shaking his head and feet, Joe Kilty warmed up his old fiddle until his music made crazy the dancers' feet, while Picquet's calls seemed to be a part of the dance. In that happy throng, gay and pleasant-hearted, there was one who was easily queen. Had old or young been asked who should reign, without a word of discontent they would have said Genevieve, while on her part she would have been just as glad if some other of her girl friends had been named.

After the dance Genevieve hurried to assist Anna at the house—Anna, who could not be persuaded to leave her kitchen longer than an hour at a time, and who fretted during that time for all the ills that the dogs could do in that short absence.

"You need not have come, dear," said Anna, "there is not much to do. Just a bit of cleaning, that's all. Stay in the hall and enjoy yourself; if I want you I'll send word by Napoleon. The Père is going to Bergeron's; it seems that Mary's a bit worse. What a smart girl that was, as quick on her feet as a woodpecker! Dance! she could dance all day and not feel it. Kilty used to say she was full of music, and all he had to do was to draw it out with the bow. But those times are gone, and more's the pity for you, Mary. Did you see Louis Frechette?—just went out as you came in. He tells me that there will be rich folk coming this afternoon to see what kind of a thing a country picnic is. It seems that Louis is guiding a party at Meacham's. I think he said there were but four in the party now, the rest had gone to New York—the father and the mother and two sons. Young men at that. Louis was telling them of the picnic and asked a day's leave, as he wished to be with his young ones to-day; so says one of the sons to his father, 'It would be worth our while to go with Louis and see what kind of a set these country folks be. I'm sure,' says he, 'that they're too funny for anything.' Louis says that whatever the boys say goes, for the father thinks they are angels, but by Louis' account they're everything but that. Louis didn't want them, but what could he do? It was as much as his job was worth to open his mouth, so they came along. They heard so much about Buttons and his yarns that they had to go into the post-office and set him a-going, an easy matter; but to stop him will tax them. Louis says they're so rich that they don't know how to spend their money. Perhaps, seeing we are so poor, and trying to fix the church, they might do honor to themselves by leaving us a bit of their plenty. I wish I was rich; if I was, poor Père would not have to be helping to cut down logs and drawing them for his church. I would make my pocket-book attend to that end of the business. Wishes are no good. It's queer what an idea of us these city folks have; they think we are all half-cracked. I'm thinking they'll find us as natural as they be. But here comes Napoleon, and it's better to be quiet. If he hears a word he'll never stop until he worms the whole story out of you. I suppose he's after more lemons. I could make three tubs of what that fellow fools away on one. It's no wonder folks vote him in every year to make lemonade, they know it's bound to be strong. If you say anything it's 'Anna, you never travelled,' or 'When I was a-soldiering.' Whist! he's at the door."

"More lemons, Anna, and as fast as you can. I want to pour it into them while they are dry. They drank the tub in a hurry, and are calling for more. Don't you hear them? 'Never drank such lemonade in my life; better than my soft stuff,' says Weeks. Hurry up, Anna, with the lemons; if you had travelled you would have learned to make hay while the sun shines. I must bring you over a pitcher of the rare juice of tub number two. When I was soldiering I learned the art. What are you keeping V. here for? are you afraid that somebody will steal her? I tell you there is danger. Buttons and Frechette have just come with two New York dandies, straw men, that live because they have a father. Frechette introduced them to me in a whisper. Poor Louis! he never travelled. Stay-at-home birds, I tell ye, don't know anything. I showed them by speaking loud enough for them to hear me that their sleek faces, fine clothes, and parental jewels didn't bewilder me a bit, not a bit. I shot better game; these fellows would run. Poor Frechette! but I suppose a job comes handy for him, and to keep such as he has it's necessary to bow and bend and play puppet. Eternal Jupiter! Anna, when are you going to get around with those lemons? Give me the basket. Come, Genevieve, and leave our old granny to have her nod."

Genevieve had the weakness of her sex, curiosity. She was glad to take up Napoleon's plea and make it her own.

"Yes, Anna, have a little nod. You must be tired. I'll just run over and dance another set or two, and by that time you will be refreshed. Just take a little snooze, and you won't miss me until 1 am here again."

"Well, just as you say, dear," said the accommodating Anna as she carefully settled herself in the easy-chair, putting the cat in her lap and rocking herself to sleep.

"She's good for the afternoon," remarked Napoleon, "unless a thunder-storm comes up, or the dogs take a notion to give her a call, then her whole body will become lively. Come, put haste to your feet. You can see the city swells from here."

Eager as was Napoleon to reach his tubs, he was overmatched by those who wished to drink his cool lemonade.

With his many assistants it took little time to have a new tub ready. Among the first to refresh themselves were Louis Frechette and his two young hunters, whom Louis introduced, much to Napoleon's disgust, to "Miss Genevieve" as Captain James Dade Fortune and Chichester Fortune. The voluble Louis was pleased to say, much to the delight of the crowd, that "these young gentlemen were sons of the Hon. James Fortune, of New York, of whom everybody has heard in one way or another. I told them," he continued, "that we were going to have a little time down here, a bit of diversion; so they spoke of it to their father, a very strict, religious man, but the best fellow in the world; and as he thinks what Captain James does is just right, so here we be to have a sup of your lemonade, Napoleon. Boys, this is my treat. Gather around. Help yourselves. It's all for a good purpose." When Frechette's treat had passed, the Captain tossed Napoleon a gold piece and bade him treat everybody. "Empty the tub as fast as you can and make more."

At this liberality there were not a few who gathered around Frechette, complimenting him for bringing along such hearty spenders.

He, always unwilling to be silent when some one was ready to listen, shrewdly observed that it was a good thing it was lemonade. If it was something stronger—something that his hunters liked better, they might be glad to get rid of them.

While women and children hurried from the hall to refresh themselves at the Captain's expense, Genevieve, at the Captain's request, was leading the way to the place of amusement, showing her kindness and politeness to a stranger. A girl looking at them over her shoulder said to her beau: "That's quite a good-looking fellow, but there's something sissy about him that I don't like. He's as much at home with Genevieve as if he knew her a lifetime. Surely she wouldn't take to him, but good clothes and wealth and talk set folks crazy these days."

Her admirer was too busy pleasing her to trouble about any other maid, and so the conversation on that subject dropped there.

"You will give me the pleasure of a dance, Miss Monnier?" said the Captain as they sat in one of the corners of the hall. "I am delighted that I accompanied Louis, who, by the way, promised me a partner for the dance. Fortune is my name, and fortune has favored me in meeting you here. I always like to choose my own partner, and, with thanks to Louis, I prefer you, Miss Monnier, as my partner for the evening. I trust you will not refuse me. If you have any notion that way remember I am a stranger, and to tell the truth a little bashful. My brother there—see, he is in the midst of fun—can put forth no such plea. What a beautiful place this is in summer, but how dreary in winter! We are delighted with the Adirondacks during these months, but Florida or Europe is much more comfortable in winter. Have you ever been in New York? There is only one New York in the world; that is my opinion, and I find it pretty well confirmed by those who have travelled. They say see Venice and then die, but I say see New York and live there the rest of your life. I asked an old fellow once who was actually starving, and who was promised work in the country, why he didn't go there, and he replied that it was better to starve in New York than live in the country in luxury. Some truth in his remark, I assure you."

"I should like to see New York," began Genevieve, timidly. "I have heard so much about it, and read so much in the papers. Yes; it must be a wonderful place. I would fear being lost in its long streets. I have a friend there, and she is surely an illustration of your remark about once seeing it and then settling there. When she left here, it seems to me so long ago, she was to come back soon, every year. I cannot tell you how many promises she made, but she has not returned, and now I know she will not, as she has lately married. If one does not care to come when one is single it is not likely that one's desire will be increased by marriage. As soon as she became acquainted, made friends, and knew where to find the amusements that attracted her, the country and its few allurements were tame—they lost the power they once had to give enjoyment."

"I don't think, Miss Monnier, that you can in your heart blame her. I believe you would do the same if in her position. I cannot see how one of your talent can hope to remain here, Miss Monnier. I assure you we need you in the city, where your worth would be appreciated. I do not speak in any wise to offend, but really the people here are crude and ignorant. They must be wearisome. Louis, for example, has no ideas beyond the woods and the things that run wild there, and I understand that he is smarter than the average. Just think what punishment it would be to have to pass one's lifetime with a Louis; and the chances, if you remain here, are you will have hundreds worse than my guide to please and put up with. I hear that the Père is a smart man, but, if he is, I wonder what keeps him in such a forsaken place as this. He must be a little peculiar, to say the least."

"Captain, you must not say anything about the Père," said Genevieve, evidently nettled, "for I fear my politeness might desert me if you did. New York may have many things, but she has no brighter nor better man than Père Monnier. Ruth discovered that long ago, and Ruth is not given to praise unless there is reason for doing so. The Père has travelled over the world. Napoleon, who has been a soldier in many countries, and who knows a great deal about the Père, says that he comes of a distinguished family, and surely the companionship of such a man cannot be called a punishment. I can understand why he remains here, simply because he was sent here by those who are his superiors, and like a true soldier he will remain until he is recalled. Then he loves his people, and I think where love is there also will happiness be found. I know he is perfectly happy."

"Miss Monnier, pardon me," said the Captain. "You really misunderstand me. I would not for the world have you think that I imputed any but the highest motives to your pastor. By the word 'peculiar' I meant to say that it was strange in one of such ability to remain here. I hardly know, now, if I express my meaning, but I assure you it would be far from my desire to say anything in the slightest reflecting on a minister of the Gospel. Of that be assured. My father is president of the Society for the Diffusion of the Bible to the natives of some place in Africa. I cannot just recollect the name. You know those African names are so long. A few of them would make a book. My good old gray grandmother, bless her old sweet heart! equips at her own expense—positively at her own expense—an evangelist to the Mexicans. She is on that subject, betimes, a little wearisome to us who are so much younger and, as she says, giddier. No, no! I could not be taken to mean any allusion to any preacher. Of that I assure you, Miss Monnier. All ministers do good in their way—are a kind of police force. I do not doubt but life and property would be in a bad way if this priest were not here. Father says priests are useful to keep in their place the poor, who would, I assure you, make life hot for us. Already the poor—a lot of scamps—are agitating and giving trouble. Father once said that if New York will ever be secure it will be when the Irish are banished from it, as these people are very troublesome."

"Oh, I don't know much of the Irish," broke in Genevieve. "Père Monnier likes them because they build all the churches and convents. I'm sure they do their share around here. We have only a few families, but they are generous to a fault, often, I think, too much so. What is given so freely is never thoroughly appreciated. As far as I have heard—what little I have heard comes from Ruth—it would be quite an undertaking to banish the Irish from New York, and I don't see why they have not as good a right to be there as other foreigners."

"I am afraid you do not desire to understand me, Miss Monnier. I was just quoting my father, who was very kind to them, but whom they turned against in the most disgraceful manner. I am sure, personally, I have met some of them who were very entertaining. I very rarely come in contact with them. To change the subject, which is not entertaining, might I ask if you are not lonesome here? I'm coming to what started our conversation. I think you should long to see some of the world. I am never weary of travel. I hope you will come some day to New York. I should be delighted to place my services at your disposal. I believe I can be trusted to show my native city off in a way it will not suffer."

"Thank you, Captain. I shall, if in New York, be delighted to make you my guide, if Ruth will permit me. I must be under her wing, otherwise the Père would never consent to my going."

"Who is Ruth I hear you talk so much about?"

"A friend of mine who was brought up here; in fact, my old school-teacher, Captain, who has lived in your city for some time. She was married a few weeks ago to an editor named O'Connor, a paragon of all perfection, so says Ruth—and who has a right to know better?"

"Charlie O'Connor! 'Tenement O'Connor' as he is called? the editor of *The Lookout*—the fellow that wrote the 'Tales of a Court,' from which he got his name? I am sorry for your friend. I know the fellow well, an arrant coward, a dangerous man. It would not be well to speak that man's name in my father's presence, the bitterest opponent he has, I believe. It is not so many years since that fellow was walking on his uppers—that's a way we have of designating poverty. Now he is a power, and a most dangerous man. No man in politics but fears his sting. I am sorry for your friend. I trust he will be more companionable to her than he generally is;

I trust so, but, as you say, she knows best. I hear the set called. What a voice that man has! I claim you as a partner."

Captain Fortune led Genevieve to her place. Picquet gave the call. Kilty, seeing a stranger, gave his bow a few extra flourishes and the dance was on.

Said Frechette as he drained the last glass in the third tub: "All eyes are on them. You would think they were made for each other."

"What are you talking about?" asked Napoleon. "What eyes? Who are made for one another?"

"Why, Genevieve and the Captain, Napoleon. I never saw in my life two dancers so graceful on a floor as they be. You would think they were a pair of swallows, so light they go it."

"Don't talk any more that stuff. Mind my tub until I get some more lemons," said Napoleon, hurriedly running to the kitchen, awakening Anna by his kicking and muttering.

"Well, faith, you must have given them some concoction to make them dry, if you are after lemons again," spoke the sleepy-looking Anna.

"Don't bother me about lemons, Anna. I have more to trouble me," said Napoleon, looking fierce. "Genevieve, that was to come back right away (you have been sleeping, Anna, nigh three hours), is over at the hall without a thought of returning, dancing and listening to that deceitful, cunning devil from

New York that Frechette calls a captain. He's as much a captain as I am. That youngster a captain! Heaven preserve me, but men must be scarce! I forgot; anything in this country can have any title for the putting on. I'll bet my old shoes that he will be a general before he's thirty. He might just as well; it's as easy to carry general as captain. I don't care what he is. I don't like him, and I tell you, Anna, I have travelled and know a thing or two. I know that V. should be over here, and I want you to make some excuse and bring her from the hall. If you don't you'll regret it. I tell you, Anna, our girl is not safe with captains; she's too young. Make some excuse."

"Get away, Napoleon, and don't be foolish," said Anna. "The child is having a good time, and you begrudge it to her. You ought to be ashamed of yourself. The poor child cannot have one day in the year without your grumble. I'll make no excuse. Just leave her there as long as she will stay. What does she care about boys? Less than I do, and that's not much. Don't go near her with your ugly face; let her have one day's fun in peace. She's only a child; a bit of a child. It's a pity you can't make an old woman of her. Here's your lemons. Do try and mind your own concern, Mr. Napoleon."

Napoleon, with many misgivings, went to his tub. Anna again sought rest in her easy-chair, and the merry dance went on.

CHAPTER XI.

OUT OF THE DEPTHS. LIGHT.

"IT is lonesome—so lonesome! Just like death. Well, in a way it is death," said Anna over the evening meal, hot tears chasing one another down her face-wrinkles. "I'll never be like myself again, and as to the Père, his system is mortally broke forever. Iron couldn't stand such a twitch as he's got. I wish she had never come to us. Not but she was, aye, good whatever madness has gone into her—the madness of death, I cannot doubt it. I wonder has he any news from her. I cannot sleep until I hear something. Little I thought what was coming; but it's over now."

Napoleon, who was sitting by the stove, his head bowed down, raised it, showing tears that would not be pent.

"Anna," said he, "I was just thinking it's just six weeks to-night since that scoundrel of a captain broke up our peace and stole poor little V. Anna, I'll never forgive myself that I did not pop that fellow the second or third time I saw him around. I might just as easy as not have peppered him with the full of your hand of lead slugs. They would have kept him picking the rest of his days. I warned you at the time of the picnic, but my talk does not go for much in this house. If it had been heeded we would not have such a sad house to-day. Anna, you can't expect to have the understanding of people that travels. I took his measure in a jiffy. I met his class before, that I did, and a mighty bad class it is. But what use to talk of what might have been done to the cage when the bird is flown?"

"Aye, and flown never to come back—never! God look to her; that's from my heart. Yes, Napoleon, travelled folks be more knowing. I didn't think of any harm, no more than the man in the moon. Bless my soul, but I'm a stupid old granny! I suppose anybody but myself would have known that something was going on by her talk. After the first few times he met her, sure there was nothing in her head but dress, and that's always a bad sign. It was the Captain said this and that and the other thing, perfectly ridiculous; but never a thing came to my old head. Could anybody think she would get such things in her head? It's true, what they say, that love is madness. Aye, marry in haste and repent at your leisure. God look to them that does so. I wonder if they're married? I heard from Frechette that Squire Butler, of Dryburgh, tied the knot."

"Eternal Jupiter!" shouted Napoleon. "Anna, are you going out of your head entirely? Where in thunder has the wisdom God has given you gone? Our V. married by Butler! That's as much a marriage as if the St. Bernard there sat as he's doing now on his hunkers and made a few passes at them with his paw. Anna, your skull is cracked since V. has gone, or you wouldn't be talking such nonsense. Didn't you know there was excommunicating for that sort of talk? Why *didn't* I empty a charge of slugs into that fellow? That's what I'm asking myself this blessed minute. Butler marrying them! Frechette has no sense. But how could you expect it? The man has never travelled. I tell you, Anna, it's the travelling business that makes the man."

"Well, Napoleon," and Anna cried bitterly, "she's lost to us—lost the same as dead, but worse. If I knew she was dead, then I would know she was out of suffering; but as it is I'm in sorrow, for who knows what's become of her? I have a little bit of money, if I only knew where she is, that I could send it to her on the quiet. I wonder would Ruth look her up."

"Anna," said Napoleon, "the talk to be sure is that the scoundrel took her to New York; but nobody is sure. Even if he did, it would not be so easy as you think to find her. It's not in this town you are when you land in New York. You might walk and walk there for weeks and not come to a bit of grass ; streets and streets ; houses and houses, one after the other; nothing but bricks. I have a fear on me that came some time ago with a dream that the villain may leave her, and if he does in a city like New York—but I hate to think of it!"

Napoleon arose to get some fire-wood. Anna muttered: "I see we can do nothing for her only to pray that nothing hurts her. I wonder where she is to-night?"

Her question caught the ears of Napoleon, and he repeated her words: "I wonder where she is to-night?"

It was an incident that while these two old servants were chatting, the one on whom their thoughts were bent was walking the streets of the great city.

Genevieve, pale and worn, shabbily dressed, with a startled air in her face, was loitering along Forty-seventh Street, seeing house after house and nothing but brick.

She had just touched the street from a dark-looking, filthy-smelling hall, just hurried from an almost unfurnished room down the creaking, railless stairs. The house from which she came was a plain brick building, built for comfort, and was, in its day, eminently respectable, but that day had long passed. The broken stone steps, the rusty iron railing, the faded doors, the rag-stuffed window-panes, and, above all, its denizens, told in plain language its story.

There was, however, evident merriment in the house, despite the appearance of squalor and poverty, as was shown by the loud laughter and frolic of the negroes and whites who mixed indiscriminately. These were its occupants. Here and there on its walls was a sign telling of a room to rent. How could any human being take up his abode there? might be asked by those who have comfortable homes, and have never even touched the fringe of misery. There are degrees of misery, and to those in the lowest degree its aspect would be palatial. It all depends on the point of view, and that is influenced by the pocketbook. Genevieve's pocketbook was light; there was not enough in it to pay for another week's rent, and the old week had just expired, so she had sought the street without any plans, rather than listen to the cross, cutting tongue of the landlady threatening police and courts, which spoke horror to this country-bred girl.

The city's noises, the whirl of the trains, the heavy thud of the dray-carts returning home, the short snort of the boring-engines on a neighboring street, the rattle of street-cars, the yelping of curs, and, above these, the thousand ways the human voice entered her ears, terrified her, making her heart annoy her with its loud beats, and her feet totter, giving her the appearance of a woman sick unto death. The smells —how different from her native air, so full of life and laughter!—seemed like a heavy weight on her head, bending it down: smells of gas, of vegetables, of dried fish, of decay, of disease, of death, met her at every footstep. On she went, nigh helpless in flesh and broken in spirit, past house after house, past sorrow and joy, her thoughts on her far-away mountain home, the memory of its love and peace, now past forever, stinging her restless soul to madness. As she passed a street-corner a hand touched her shoulder, and, startled, she turned to meet a woman's face, once beautiful, as a glimpse would tell, but deeply ravaged by the sorrow-poison with which the arrow-points of unholy living are tipped.

"You're new on this beat," said the stranger, throwing sympathy into her voice. "It's the first time I've seen you. What do they call you? You're not new to the city, are you?"

They were now under the full glare of the street-lamp, and the stranger continued: "My, but you're young and pretty! I hate to see you on the streets, but I suppose you are driven here like the rest of us. Can't you walk a bit quicker—just a little bit? If you don't I fear the cop on the next corner may make it lively for us. Just see! he's getting a gait on him and coming this way! Better come this way with me and let him pass," and the strange woman, grasping the arm of the dreaming girl, rather pulled than led her through a dark hallway, to a room brilliantly lighted, where men and women sat by small circular tables, laughing, talking loudly, smoking, singing, drinking frothy beer from huge mugs. The eyes of Genevieve in a moment swept the motley crew, reckless in their *abandon;* a sense of shame, cold, and griping passed through her. Then came the strength of other days, nerving her for the struggle. The voice of her companion was coarse, her face full of unwomanly blotches, the whole company a set of leering devils. She fancied she could hear distinctly the sweet voice of Père Monnier, and, through the blur of her tears, his tall form arose in cassock and surplice, his eyes lit up, and his right arm at full stretch pointing at her. It was the old message he had so often announced from the altar of his own little church in the days when his voice was heaven to Genevieve: "The wages of sin is death."

"Death—death!" she hissed. "I smell the decay." Then: "Blessed voice, that led my childhood, speak to my heart in this hour of my sorrow. I have sinned; I will suffer; but let not my wages be death."

"What are you muttering about?" said the stranger. "You look as if you were going out of your senses. Your eyes are mad. Why don't you sit down and take things easy?"

"Take things easy!" almost screamed Genevieve. "Find delight in hell? The wages of sin, I know, is death." And, without knowing which way she hurried, she was soon on the street, wondering how it was that the tottering of her feet and the snapping of her heart had passed away.

The city's day sounds were dying out as she approached Fifth Avenue. The sight of its lights and the prancing, well-groomed, silver-harnessed horses that rattled up and down its length, bearing luxury, speaking of all things that money may do, brought vividly to her mind how near poverty may lie to riches, and yet how far. A laughing couple, evidently out for a walk on the avenue, passed her at quickstep; the woman, as they did so, turning her head and looking into her face hurriedly, then whispering something to her companion. Genevieve held back while the man and woman, who held a rapid conversation, stopped, the woman with an evident intention of returning and addressing her—an intention which so frightened Genevieve that she quickly retraced her steps and turned down another street, followed part way by the strange couple. When she was safe from them a thought came that the woman's form and walk were familiar, but probe her sick head as she would no name would come to her tongue.

"If they knew me once," she muttered, "when I was myself, it is just as well that they should not know me now. They would ask so many questions, and how could I answer them? Oh, dear me! I have sorrow enough now. If any more comes I will just lie down and die."

The sound of music recalled Genevieve from her black thoughts and her plaintive mutterings, recalled her to the fact that she was on the streets of the great city, poorly clad, almost penniless, and on these streets she, who had been nurtured so tenderly, must pass the night. "And what a night!" came to the mind of this country-bred girl, as all the dreadful tales she had heard of the great city darted across her mind. Robbers, thieves, criminals of every class and kind would lurk in every alley-way seeking the unwary, robbing them of their money, maybe out of pure devilment killing them.

For the first time in her life ghosts were less to be dreaded than men. She did not know that it was fear of man that first begot fear of ghosts. Should she keep on walking street after street, taking care that her walking was in those that were well lighted and, as she thought, less liable to be the haunts of the wicked, or should she seek some unpretending tenement and there, in the name of Him who is Father to all, ask for shelter only?

Genevieve thought that only in the haunts of the poor would compassion be granted to her misery. It is useless to ask by what process of the mind this unsophisticated country-girl came to think so. Her thought is common even to wiser heads. She could not decide from whence it came, so she hurrried on, the music becoming more and more distinct. Her fine ear told her at once that the music was rough, jagged, and out of tune, yet there was something human, something fascinating about it. The musicians were in earnest. It was more by dint of blowing than by science that the brass rang out a message. The drum had a welcome rattle, noisy, it was no doubt, but delightfully chummy. As the music ceased, Genevieve, whose heart it had warmed, listened, impatient for more, but instead there came in a rough voice these words:

> "Tho' your sins be as scarlet,
> They shall be as white as snow.
> Hear the voice that entreats you.
> Oh! return you unto God;
> He'll forgive your transgressions
> And remember them no more."

The text from Isaias, which was the base of their song, was familiar to her ears from childhood, as the text that Père Monnier loved to quote when preaching on his favorite subject, penance. Again his form rose before her, no longer cold and stern, no longer driving her away, but by soft, sweet speech asking her to return, reminding her that if the Master forgave, what was man that he should hold wrongs forever in his heart?

How she wished for the wings of a bird to bear her back to her mountain home! Père Monnier's forgiveness meant that of Napoleon and Anna, and with them happiness would come again. Her future life should be a reparation for the past.

Turning the first corner came a number of men and women, their features lighted up by a huge torch which blazed in their centre. It was from them that the music and song came. She joined them as a short, thick-set man took off his cap and in a harsh voice began to preach. The harangue, for by no latitude could it be called a sermon, was cold and commonplace, interspersed with ejaculations and tambourine-shakings. It had none of the warmth of the music; it could not touch like the song. When he had finished, a peculiarly bonneted woman took his place—a woman whose face, lighted by the torch, was striking. It might once have been beautiful, but now it was drawn, sorrow-stitched, neither inviting nor repulsive, a face which the eye marks but speech cannot describe. As she did so, in rich full voice came her song whose burden was, " Come to Jesus."

What peculiar associations will not the mind produce! Curiously enough that voice reminded Genevieve of the first March robin, on the spray of a bare maple, singing of spring and luring a partner for the pleasant weather. When the song was finished the captain, in a few pleasant words, invited the crowd to accompany them to their headquarters and " hear more music and, above all, the Gospel." Then the cheery music broke forth and they tramped away to its sound. A few heeded the invitation, but the majority, laughing and commenting on their amusement, went on to find new things to invite their attention. The singer remained, and, when the crowd had passed, drew near to Genevieve, clasping her hand and whispering in her ear:

"Sister, I know you are in sorrow. What ails you? Are you homeless? friendless? I know you are a stranger, a little country-girl, allured to the city like a moth to a light. Return, child! There is nothing in this world can save you if you remain here. I know it. I know it. While I sang I watched your face, and I have learned that lesson, child, which is not at all difficult to know, through the face—the sorrows that eat the heart. How young you are! Just at an age when you should have as much care as a bird, and—don't feel annoyed at me, child— sorrow is leeching the blood out of your face and misting your eyes. God knows what it has done to your heart. There is only one way to get rid of the pest, only one way, dear, and that is to return to your home. I was just thinking, while I was singing and looking at you—looking at you, I say, child: you looked, too, so lovely—how glad would some household be to have you, what welcomes they would give! Joy, nothing but joy! Yet here you are, and not a friend. Now, this must not be; you must return home and beg forgiveness, for it will be easily given. You cannot remain in this big, devouring city to be trampled and torn and worn to death, and then thrown into potter's field, like the way we bury beasts in the country. You must not cry, I say, but be strong and good, as I know you are, and follow my advice and return. Money? No thought of that! I can beg enough for your ticket. Now here is a little, just a trifle, and a card. Get a place to sleep at once, and the card will tell you my address, and bright and early you will come and see me, and what a nice little chat we shall have! Now you must do all these things, and remember, darling, 'The wages of sin is death.'"

The singer hurried away, followed by the grateful eyes of Genevieve. She would have lovingly thanked her benefactor, but, struggle as she would to master speech, no words would come to her tongue, so she watched and watched until the noble-hearted woman was lost to her view; tnen clutching the coin and card she kept on aimlessly walking, constantly repeating, "The wages of sin is death."

Try as she might to banish it, the text ran through her brain, but how to analyze it or find its meaning Genevieve knew not. It brought the idea of fear of punishment in the future. Yet was she not punished enough? and if the kind lady would send her to her mountain home there would be, she assured herself, despite the heart-break she had been, nothing but joy. So she reasoned in her helpless, girlish way, bringing plausible reasons to settle her mind; but the text brought a mystery, and, like all mysteries, it would not be put down.

Without noticing it she had come to a narrow, dimly lighted street, and the tales of ill flocking to her mind drove her quickly to a better lighted street, which soon led to Fifth Avenue.

She read the name on the lamp-post, and felt a few twitches of gladness pass through her, as she touched for the first time the street made well known to her by Ruth's long descriptions.

In front of her was a magnificent church, reaching with its tall spires, she fancifully thought, the sky and its clear shining stars. This must be the Cathedral, of whose size and beauty she had often heard, one of the sights that Ruth had promised to show her when she would come on that long-promised visit. It was strange that hundreds of miles from her home all things should suggest it. Some influence that she could not explain made her cross the street and stand before the great door, afraid to enter, loath to pass on. Like a little child, with a mixture of curiosity and fright, she softly pushed the great split door and it gave little by little, until it opened on the vestibule; then she crept in, and through the slight baize doors stole heavenly music. At the sound she panted like the long-run deer of her mountain home as he throws himself into the cool brook. Lost to his ears is the noise of his tormentor as he licks the crystal water. That music so delicious, so grand, and yet so homely in the sense of creeping around and hushing her heart! How well she knew that hymn! how often she had sung it in the olden days! The little church on the top of the hill, the Salmon River, a silver thread tying the little valley to the wood-crowned Adirondacks, came to her memory. Yes; that little church, with its little altar, so sweet-smelling, decorated with new-cut clover-blossoms, buttercups, daisies, and the bunching dogwood, came to her by the magic touch of music. That hymn! What memories it brought now! She listened as the choir sang:

> '*Tantum ergo Sacramentum*
> *Veneremur cernui:*
> *Et antiquuum documentum,*
> *Novo cedat ritui:*
> *Præstet fides supplementum,*
> *Sensuum defectui.*"

In her love of the music she had pushed wider than she meant the baize door. Far away was the altar, a mass of light and flowers. On her tiptoes she entered and sank on her knees, smelling the incense with delight, allowing her eyes to be ravished with the stained glass, glowing itself with altar light, while the choir sang, sweeter and holier she thought:

> "*Genitori, Genitoque,*
>   *Laus et jubilatio,*
>   *Salus, honor, virtus, quoque.*
>   *Sit et benedictio:*
>   *Procedenti ab utroque*
>   *Compar sit laudatio.*"

The coped priest, with a little lamb and a cross richly wrought in gold and silver on the back of the cope—a symbol which caught Genevieve's eye and made her reason herself a little lamb clinging to the cross—in rich voice sang:

> "*Panem de cælo præstitisti eis.*"

At his voice Genevieve's eyes looked to the altar, and her heart filled with prayer to Him who suffered little children to flock around Him. The music died away, the candles, like stars dropping behind dawn, went out one by one, the stained glass was dark, the robed priest and his fair-faced youths gone, the worshippers departed, but Genevieve's eyes still faced a twinkling red light, that threw a strange glamour over the great high altar, and her weary heart was drawing comfort from Him who told the parable of the lost sheep. The burden of her prayer was the one which the sorrow-pressed ever wring from their hearts— rest, only rest!

When the sacristan touched her on the shoulder, and in gentle tones, reminding her of Napoleon, said, "When you are done with your devotions, lady,"

Genevieve, strong of faith and full of hope and courage, feeling that the Lord would direct her, and believing that those who are under His guidance need have no fear, arose, gave the old man a smile, and went out into the pleasant night air, confident of soon finding a sleeping-place. She had walked only a block when the sound of music again fell on her ear, but how different from what she had heard ! a kind of feeble drone, grinding out a popular song. Genevieve stopped short a moment, wondering whether her ears were not playing her some trick. But no; the music was certainly at the corner; what could it be at this time of night ? But in a large city there are so many strange things that she felt she ought not to be astonished. So she went on until she reached the corner of the street, and there, sitting on the pavement, the lamp-post at her back, was the musician, an old woman, huddled in a heap, grinding out a song; a few lead-pencils in her hand, and a little tin cup on the pavement to hold the pennies her feeble music brought. Her clothes, faded in color, were neatly arranged, her whole appearance one of cleanliness. Her face was still fresh and inviting; the only trace of rancor lay in the snapping black eyes, which moved with a curious alertness. I do not know whether science has recorded it, but it is a fact that a man-hunted dog will wear the misuse in his eyes.

This old musician turned mechanically the crank of her music-box, and when no passer-by approached her tin cup, hummed a tune different from that of the box to keep her company. It was evident that she was well known, for a policeman crossed the street to joke with her and chat of his family.

As the guardian of the law sang out, "Safe home, Sal," and the old musician put the tin cup in her huge pocket preparatory to her home-going, Genevieve came close to her with a hearty "Good-night." The old lady pleasantly nodded her head, and putting the music-box under her arm, arose and looked her young well-wisher straight in the face.

"It's a beautiful night," said the old woman, "beautiful as it can be; but whatever is the reason, there was no crowd on the streets. It was very quiet."

"Oh, my!" said Genevieve, "I thought the streets were full. They surely are not much more crowded, are they?"

"God bless your wit, dear, is that all you know? If that was going to be the case I might go out of business. You're not a New Yorker or you wouldn't be astonished at anything. Are you going my way? I turn down the next street. This street is sacred to the millionaires, the leeches, blast them! It's coming near to the time when their heads will roll in the gutter. What we want is a revolution—

smash! Charlie O'Connor promised me that it was bound to come, and it will come. I tell ye, youngster, it will come! I'm pretty old, more from hardships than from age, but I expect to live long enough to have a hand in the smash. I turn here. Do you hear the music in the corner house? Fine, is it not? Listen to their laughing and their antics. The owner of that house came over in the same ship with me, as poor as a church-mouse—a poorhouse boy. I took so much pity on him that I gave him bread and tea, and God knows what else! Now he wouldn't walk on the same side of the street with me. I came over with him on the *Blackbird*, and here I am, grinding a box on the street every night for a iving, and he's living on fat and robbing creation. He made all his money out of the Irish—out of me and the likes of me. But he has no use for us now. I hear he calls himself Scotch or some other outlandish name. But it won't work unless he cuts his tongue out, and then his face would convict him. Bad and all as he is, I don't hate him half so bad as his mother-in-law. She's the villain for you. I could spawl on her, the crocodile! I mind when I came to the country she was mistress of a saloon in whose floor you could walk bog deep in the sawdust. Then she had a Mc to her name, and none of the nonsense she's full of to-day. She had one of the best husbands that ever lived, but when he died the fooling began, and they're the laughing-stock of everybody. They put poor fools in the madhouse, but rich fools can run around; everybody wants to be their keeper. Some people are born lucky. Just think of that tow-headed workhouse boy owning this house, and I, that come from the best stock, having permission to sit on the pavement."

The old woman was silent, as if turning over the past.

"I would like to ask you a question," said Genevieve, "before we part."

"Ask it, dear," said the other impatiently. "No excuses to be made to Sal McClintock, not a one. I'm used to answering questions. What is it? Out with it, dear, for it's getting late. I always had one fault. Start me to talk and I never know when to stop—never. Pop your question."

"I am a stranger in the city," said Genevieve. "I have no friends; not one. I have little money, very little, and if you could direct me to some place of shelter for the night I would pray for you. Yes, indeed I would; that is my only way to recompense you, Mrs. McClintock."

"I don't want you, dear, to put any of your airs to my name. If you want to get along with me call me Sal. Around these diggings for years I go by the name of Old Sal, and my ears have kind of taken to it, so you might as well follow the rest."

"Old Sal, then," said Genevieve, "do you know where I could get lodgings near? I feel so tired. A country-girl needs practice to walk your pavements."

"Aye," said Sal, "that's true as you're standing there. You're a little country-girl. I know that the first glimpse I had; nothing forward about you. Yes, a country-girl! But, dear, that's where you should be to-night, instead of in this miserable place.

"When I came here from Ireland I went to the country in Connecticut, but I made a fool of myself, and, despite my sister's advice, married a worthless fellow who was a kind of showman over home, and the devil was in his feet. He could never give his toes rest, until he would come to New York. Then he seemed satisfied to pass the rest of his life fighting and drinking, while I had to make the living, and nothing soft about the way I had to make it, scrubbing on my hands and knees, from the break of day until night. I had a few children, but the Lord knew better than me, so He took them—praise be to His holy will! What He does is for the best. They're a good deal better off to-night than their poor old mother. Rob was a long time sick, so I had to earn our living and attend him, which soon broke me up. After his death a gathering came in my side and put an end to my washing and scrubbing, and drove me to this Italian business. Little did I think when I left Ireland that I would ever be in the monkey-men's business. If Rob had only stayed in the country we might have been happy and had our children. But what use in talking? He's dead, poor fellow! and I hope in peace. Rob wasn't bad-hearted, but he had no sense. My, how he hated the fellow that owns this house! As I told you, we all came over in the ship together, and we were all just as thick with one another as butter. When the fellow run for office, Rob was out day and night looking up votes. He got a cold that he never got rid of, in that election, but when Rob asked him for some light job he pretended that he didn't know him, and as Rob was as proud as a peacock, he turned on his heel and never bothered the upstart again. But here I'm telling you my tales when it's home I should be and in my bed fast asleep."

"What you say interests me," said Genevieve, trying to please; "yes, very much. But you have not answered my question."

"That's so, Miss, that's so. I'm so given to talking that once my tongue's loose there's no stopping. I know many places, but if I knew just the depth of your pocketbook it would be easy directing you. There's lodging in New York to fit all our pockets. If there was not, God pity some of us. I should not be complaining; strangers have been kinder than kith or kin. What is your name, if I am not asking too much ? If I am, don't bother your head about me or my question."

"Genevieve is my name—Genevieve Bain. I suppose you never heard of any one of that name before, yet I think it is quite a pretty name."

Old Sal mused for awhile and then replied : " I didn't, did I ? Well, I guess I did know a Genevieve, the sweetest and the most patient body I ever met. But don't let me think, dear. I'm too near the scoundrel who drove her child to the streets, another little Genevieve, I hope in heaven now—a place that the rascal will never enter unless justice is the same as down here. I'm thinking it's a kind of late to be sending you anywhere, a stranger like you ; so if you're what I take you to be, a sensible girl, you'll come along with me and put up with what I can give. It may be poor, but it's clean and not begrudged. Do you know I would rather have one potato and the tail of a salt herring, where it comes in welcome, than all the roasts and sauces and pudding you could wag a stick at, that I would. In the morning, after a good night's rest, you'll be fresh and ready to look around, but I fear you'll have a time getting anything to do. You do look so frail. I suppose it's writing work that you're after, but I'm afraid you'll find it hard to get. What's killing the country is that everybody wants it easy, and there's not enough situations of that kind on hand. I know a lady strong and full of book-learning that tried all kinds of advertisements and walked the shoes off her feet trying to get something to do, and if she had not met the kindliest of men, who not only gave her work but married her, I don't know what the poor thing would have done. Gone crazy, possibly, like many I have seen in this same city."

"O Sal! I shall be glad to go," said Genevieve, the first chance she had in the lull of Sal's story. "You are so good to take me to your home, which I assure you will be a paradise to me."

"A paradise!" continued Sal. "A poor paradise, but such as it is you're welcome to it, aye, as the Irish say (I take you to be French, dear, but you're fair), one hundred thousand times welcome. I could give you that in Irish. I'm not like the scoundrel that owns the corner. I haven't forgotten where I come from. I'm not Scotch!" And Sal laughed a wild broken laugh, so fierce that Genevieve felt a cold wave pass through her.

"A paradise!" continued Sal. "I suppose any shelter is a paradise to the homeless. Yes; the room was once a paradise to one little Genevieve long, long ago. Come, we have stood here too long; sleep is better than talk."

"Give me your music-box," said Genevieve. "I am younger; do, please, let me carry it and lighten you a bit."

The two women left the avenue, and after little less than half an hour's walking came to Sal's home, entered the open door and clambered up the stairs. A woman's deft fingers had made the room cosey. The walls were cheaply but tastefully papered, while the few chairs and the table, second-hand ones to be sure, yet comfortable, to Genevieve looked inviting. The carpet had lost or half-lost its hue, but it was free from rent and spots. The bed, an old wooden one, was covered with a snowy white spread. On the bedpost hung a rough brass crucifix. There were mugs and cups and saucers on the table, and the materials for a cold luncheon, which no sooner was the door closed than Sal prepared for her guest.

"Eat," she said, as she handed the food. "Genevieve, nourishment does no harm. Just listen! It's twelve o'clock. I hear the hours strike, but it's early for me; besides I can sleep all day, and unless you must get out early you might just as well take your ease in the morning and have a good sleep. If you have walked much, and not being used to it, I'm thinking you'll find your limbs a trifle stiff in the morning, and if you do, rest is your best ointment. Now, as soon as you eat your lunch, go to bed. Bad and all as I am, I do a little praying—just a little before I turn in for the night; it's nigher the morning I should be saying."

As Genevieve's eyes wandered around the room

they rested on two cabinet pictures, evidently, from their dazzling frames, the treasure of the room.

"I see you have pictures, Sal," said Genevieve.

"Just three, Genevieve; one of my old man when he was young, before the rheumatics twisted him like a hoop, and two more of friends. Take them down from the wall and look at 'em; they're the finest in this city."

Genevieve did as she was desired, and readily recognized that of the woman as Ruth Croydon, her old school-teacher and friend. She kept the knowledge, not without a slight tremor of her face.

"You look as if you knowed 'em," said Sal, "but I hardly think you do. That is Charles O'Connor, the editor of *The Lookout* and the man that pays my rent, and I'm not a drop's blood to him. Just an old acquaintance. When he was down in the world I used to wash for him and do his mending, so when he got up he wasn't like the rest. Says he, 'Sal, I hear Rob's dead and that you're turned to music, and making out poorly. Now,' says he, 'my old room where I sent the golden lass that brought me fortune is vacant, so I want you to occupy it and I'll pay the rent, and perhaps a little more. I have a kind of a sneaking regard for that room, Sal; it knew me when I was poor and the struggle as much as I could bear. Now I don't want any of your pride, Sal; it neither fits me nor you, nor any sensible body, so come down to-morrow and get the key, and we'll see that you're cosey.' That's what Charlie said. He has a heart in him as big as an ox. Faith, I had no capers in my head! Down I went and got the key, and here I am ever since, sure of shelter, and I might as well say food, for Charlie and his wife take a walk two or three times a week round my way and put enough in the pan to keep me alive—that they do.

"The golden lass he talks about was a little girl whose mother died, and the brute that lives on the corner turned me and the child out, and Charlie he just thought the world of the child and wrote a book about her. But what do you think did he do but give us this identical room and all the money he had and walk the streets all night! That's Charlie. I gave the child to a monkey-man, may God forgive me! but what else could I do? Rob had lost his own, and he would have no other child around. Poor Parenti! I knew him for years, and I knew him to be kind. He went to the country, and of him or the child I never heard tale or tidings after. The child must be dead; she was delicate, and no wonder at it, for she was half-starved and half-clad for a whole year afore her mother died. It makes my heart bleed to think how they rattled her mother over the stones, for all I know to be cut up by the doctors, and she came of the best stock. I'm sure you might travel all Ireland over and not find such a girl as her mother,

Judy McCrudden, was, and on the Swanton side of her there was never an Irishman landed in New York could beat him in a big heart. He was a torch of hospitality, that's what you were, John Swanton. Nobody passed your door hungry."

"How came his daughter to be so desolate?" asked Genevieve.

"That's easy telling," continued Sal. "Like many another girl she didn't know the value of a home. She was young and foolish, and easily led, and a smart, glib talker, one of your snakes, twisted himself around her heart—poisoned it, I'll warrant. She would take no advice, so up she gets and runs away and marries him. Well, she lived to repent her folly. You might as well say she killed her father, and for that matter her mother, for they lived no time after. They left property in the hands of the McDades, but all their daughter ever got out of it was the use of a room, at a reduced rate, while the poor thing lived. She was hardly cold when they hurried her off, as I was telling you, and drove me and her child into the street. That was the time that Charlie O'Connor (God be good to him!) sent us here."

"And what about the husband," said Genevieve, trying to conceal her tears.

"Husband? I don't know, Genevieve. He wasn't worth keeping track of; he left her before the baby was born, and has never been seen since, and it's not much matter, bad luck to him! I carried the baby to church and had it baptized, and helped the mother all I could, until she died, though that wasn't much. What little it was it had to be done on the quiet, as Rob was cranky and full of notions, but I suppose if he had been himself it would have been different. Anyhow, I done as well as I could. The other picture there is Mrs. O'Connor; looks just like her. That's the girl that was lucky enough to get a job and a man. She's just as fine as she looks. You might well call them a splendid pair! Only for them it's in the almshouse I would be, from which may God be between me and harm! That's the last place for the Irish. Go to bed, dear, or my tongue will wag all night."

Genevieve bent by the bedside in prayer for a few moments, and then, undressing, slipped into bed, turned her head to the wall, shut her weary eyes and, like a tired child, stretched her limbs, softly sighed and went asleep.

"Poor dear!" said Sal, bending over her and fixing the clothes to her feet. "I wonder where she comes from. Hearts are aching some place for her to-night. If the O'Connors don't go off to-day, as they said they would, as soon as I get up I'll take her to them; they might get her something to do. God bless her, anyway, and everybody's child that's far from home."

Old Sal took from the bedpost the roughly made crucifix and placed it on the bedspread; then she knelt by it and prayed that through the agony of Him who suffered for sinners she, poor and sinful, would have mercy, the O'Connors blessings, and, lastly, that God would watch her sleeping charge. Then she arose, put out her lamp, and sank in sleep beside the golden lass.

CHAPTER XII.

DISENTANGLING THE RAVEL.

WITH bowed head and serious face Napoleon stood ringing the bell of the little church on an August Sunday morning. The dogs scampered around him without the slightest recognition on his part. His usual custom of plucking a bunch of flowers for the altar, his token of love, was forgotten. The pulling of the bell-rope seemed to weary him, for his work in this line, heretofore so stately and graceful, was petulant and whimsical.

The neighbors asked one another what was up, as the bell jerked out its ragged call, and not a few held that the old soldier was absent and that some uncouth altar-boy was trying his unpractised hand.

When the bell-ringing was over, Napoleon entered the little church and knelt to pray. The bell brought Père Monnier, pale and haggard-looking, from his library into the open air. His face showed here and there plain evidence of his recent sickness, brought on, no doubt, by worry and the terrible drenching he had while attending the funeral of old Bergeron's granddaughter. The day had been so pleasant that the Père had robed but lightly; but hardly had the corpse left the house, when a drooping, coal-black cloud stole between the earth and sunshine, hushing the song-birds and bringing a strange but indefinable feeling to the mourners. Then came rain, a few beady drops, spotting the dry, warm dust, followed by sheets of water. Among those whom it drenched was the Père, who drove in front of the cortège. A good hour had to pass before his clothing could be changed, and in that time, so said the parishioners, "he had caught his sickness."

It was evident that he was glad to be around again, for, as he stood surveying his lawn, he tossed his head in a well-pleased way to catch the fragrant airs that the morning breeze brought him. His watchful eyes were scanning the flower-beds to see what were the losses and gains during his sickness.

The worshippers flocked to the church in a leisurely way, gossiping of their farms and the week's news. The young skipped about them, or scampered before them, as full of life as well-fed kittens, chattering with one another or quizzing their elders, questions which from their oddness became food for hearty laughter. Their hearts were wrapped in the little church and its pastor. Sunday was not only a day of rest for the body and sunshine for the spirit, it was more—a day of news, of kindly gossip, of visiting and of gracious entertaining. Those who came from a distance dined with those nearer the church. The parish was a family united in race and religion under Père Monnier's loving guidance. The flight of Genevieve had fallen on their ears but to provoke wrath from their mouths. They could not understand how any one could strike their pastor such a blow, above all a girl whom he, as they expressed it, "had taken off the street, dressed, and given her the bit out of his own mouth." Their speech was taxed to find words bitter enough to condemn her for the heartless action which, they argued, was the cause of the Père's sickness more than the summer shower, which was as harmless as a bath of lukewarm water.

Napoleon had given them to understand that any talk or fuss about Genevieve would be distasteful to Père Monnier. Not that the Père had said anything to make him think so. It was one of Napoleon's hobbies and boasts, as often expressed as a chance was given, that he could read the mind of any man "with just a look in his face." In his lifetime he met not a few who laughed at this and offered him a test for his powers, but, to quote from his own story, he came off easily the victor on every occasion. With his hobby he measured his master's face, and who will deny that at least on one occasion his measurement was true? The Père on his part, ignorant of the hint dropped by his faithful servant, believed that it was their love for him, and what they deemed his sufferings for the disgrace to his home, which smothered the talk.

This disgrace was to these earnest mountaineers especially keen. Genevieve, brought up in a priest's house, forgetting herself so much as to be married by a justice, which was in their eyes no marriage at all! How could the Père, they thought, be able to admonish with effect wayward members inclined like Genevieve, when one of his own household, who should have been a pillar of faith, a stay to the weak, showed herself so lacking in gratitude, so thankless and wanting? These were the family whispers after the children had gone to bed.

"It's a God-send, Père, to see you able to attend to your duties again," said Anna, hobbling into church. "But what use in you getting better, if you don't take more care of yourself? There was no call for you going up to Bergeron's and 'companying the hearse. Others more strong than you be wait for the corpse in the church, and they get as much thanks."

"That may be all true, Anna," said the Père, laughing, "all true, but I don't do those things for thanks. I look on them as duty, Anna. I am sure in this case there were thanks. Poor old Bergeron seemed to grow younger, and he assured me that my coming took off his heart a heavy load of sorrow. The rainfall did me no hurt; my sickness was some kind of a distemper that's going around, nothing more. It certainly did give me a close call, but I'm well again. I scent the air, and I have an appetite, a true sign of health. Oh! I'm to be depended on for a good many years. I won't die as long as I can help it. When I must, I must; that's all there is to it, Anna."

"Did Bergeron forgive her afore she died?" asked Anna. "I was curious to know, but I don't want to meddle in things that don't concern me. I heard that he was pretty mad, poor man! and I don't blame him much. It's trying when your own flesh and blood is a kind of foolish and crazy acting."

"We must all forgive and forget, Anna. Don't we pray for forgiveness every day, as we in turn promise to forgive? The old man long since forgave her, and by every kindness within his power proved his forgetfulness of the past. He was, whatever may have been his harshness when she first came, kind and loath to part with his little girl. He told me that he really never knew how much he loved her until he sat by her bedside day after day and watched her melting away. Her big eyes, with that strange glare that consumption shoots through them, pierced his heart. He said it was agony for him to see her lying helpless, a part of her voice cut away daily, until he had to bend over her and put his ear to her poor little dry mouth. She was patient, poor thing. Forgive her? I should say he did."

"Sure that's what we're here for," said Anna, "if folks could only get it into their heads. I hope all of us will have the grace to forgive if it ever comes our turn; that's my prayer!" And Anna, with this hint, or, as she would call it, shot at the Père, sought the church.

Père Monnier smiled at the passing form of the good old dame, noticing well that in her own crude way she was pleading the cause of the lost Genevieve. Yet, somehow or other, the thought which Anna's hint awoke was distasteful to him. He had hoped to banish all remembrance of the girl for whom he had done so much.

It was not so easy to banish Genevieve, when, as Napoleon put it, every stick and stone hummed her name.

Père Monnier, leaning on the fence, was started in thought by the words of his old housekeeper—words that he could not deny other than foundation-stones of the religion he preached so vigorously and so constantly. It was only when an acolyte in his flaming red cassock and white surplice approached him and hesitatingly touched his arm, that he was aroused from his study.

"It is a little after the time," said the boy cautiously, "just a little bit. We thought on account of your being sick that you might have forgotten."

"Very well, my boy," said the Père, as he followed the olive-skinned, big-eyed boy to the little sacristy and robed for worship. There was nothing rich or elaborate about the little mountain church. Yet many a tourist from the torturing, parched city, meeting this little sanctuary, turned from the dry, dusty highway and sought therein a quiet and holy calm he had read of but not hitherto felt. It was a place where the body was lulled to rest and eased of war, while the spirit was loosened, cleansed, and sent from out the flesh-ark to behold the olive-leaves of eternity. I hold it beyond the might of man to draw that feeling which comes to one fresh from the toil and turmoil of the world on entering such a sanctuary where everything symbolizes death, dust, and resurrection. How fleeting human time! how paltry human ambition! how profitless human fame!

It must have been in such a retreat, "far from the madding crowd," with the whisperings of nature all around and symbolism preaching, that À Kempis learned to say:

"*It is vanity also to mind this present life and not to look forward unto those things which are to come.*

"*It is vanity to love that which passeth with all speed and not to hasten thither where everlasting joy remaineth.*"

The going of the Père to the sacristy was the signal for those who loitered around enjoying their smoke to knock the ashes from their pipes and join in the devotion. As they entered and took their accustomed places the priest began the service. The choir —the organist was a simple village girl, proud of her acquirements—sang in simple, prayerful way the Mass, one of Mozart's. As Napoleon once said, this singing had none " of the frills or theatre-business of city churches " whose music distracts devotion. It was sweet, simple, and solemn, uniting with the priest's voice, blending with the prayers of the congregation, the wings on which were borne the petitions of priest and people.

When the service was over, Père Monnier, partly disrobed of his vestments, turned to his watchful flock, and from his time-worn book read softly:

"See that you despise not one of these little ones: for I say to you, That their angels in heaven always see the face of My Father who is in heaven.

"For the Son of man is come to save that which was lost. What think you? If a man have an hundred sheep, and one of them should go astray, doth he not leave the ninety-nine in the mountains, and go and seek that which is gone astray?

"And if it so be that he find it, amen I say to you, he rejoiceth more for that than for the ninety-nine that went not astray.

"Even so it is not the will of your Father, who is in heaven, that one of these little ones should perish.

"But if thy brother shall offend against thee, go and rebuke him between thee and him alone: if he shall hear thee, thou shalt gain thy brother."

Shutting the book, the Père bent his head as if to give time for the force and beauty of his text thoroughly to penetrate the hearts of his hearers, a custom to which they seemed to be habituated, for they also bent their heads as if in serious meditation on the words he had spoken. The altar-boys' faces were full of smiles and belief. Youth learns not by meditation, but by love. It is only age that needs stays.

When he looked up his eyes rested on his people in the attitude of honest attention. As his church held no pulpit, he spoke from the highest step of the altar, in a quiet way, free from gesture. His words were the simple every-day speech of his people wonderfully woven, each word well put, conveying his meaning, no more, no less, the whole bringing home to them his ideas fresh and clean-cut. The illustrations were of the homeliest kind, drawn from the familiar life around them. Speech and illustration were their own. A few touches and the sheep were seen, strolling in the green grassy valley, grazing at their will as they went; then one leaves the happy fold and wanders away from its fellows by slippery pathways, arid rocks, dangerous cliffs, on to the lonesome woods, where grow the tangled briers and thorns, where the grass is scanty, where foxes and wolves abound, whose joy is death to the sheep. The shepherd misses his sheep, and, fearful of the ills that may befall it, leaves his flock and journeys after it, seeks until he finds it, and then brings it to the fold. The shepherd was Christ; the lost lamb the sinner. Then he spoke on the love that Christ bore sinners, His quest for them, His call to a higher life, His mercy, quoting: "Though your sins be as scarlet, they shall be as white as snow." With Christ's love he contrasted man's inhumanity to man, bade his people repent, exhorted them to charity, "the fulfilling of the Law," told them that charity was a "royal law," and that they would pass from death unto life when they loved their brethren. His sermon was on love—love to the Creator, love to His noblest creation—love so beautifully described as "long-suffering, kind, modest, unassuming, innocent, simple, orderly, disinterested, meek, pure-hearted, sweet-tempered, patient, enduring."

How foolish to attempt to catch the faintest glimpses of Père Monnier's sermon, wanting his voice full of feeling, his eyes full of that light which is given only to the simple and clean of heart! When he had finished, tears coursed down his cheeks and large beads of perspiration clung to his forehead. His hearers had responded to his every word; what came from his mouth went right to their hearts, the promptings of coming deeds that would cause their dust to smell sweet. The hot tears that lay on their cheeks spoke of the emotions moving their pastor as moving them. There could be no doubt that the Père was reproaching himself with his harshness to girlish Genevieve, one of Christ's little ones. The divine Master sought out the lost sheep, but the disciple closed the paddock lest the wanderer return, thus driving it to its death in the trackless forest. What a chasm lay between the Master and the disciple! To weigh justly one's self is, of all things, the most difficult. Père Monnier, from long meditating on his daily actions, had learned this difficult art. The sermon had sunk deep into his heart. Weighed in the balance he preached, he was found wanting, and the tears in his eyes were crushed there by the wine-press of sorrow. While he taught the beautiful lessons of the Master, was not his flock contrasting his conduct in the case of Genevieve with what the Master would have done? The story of Mary Magdalen vividly held his mind, therein telling the Master's way.

"Be ye kind one to another, merciful." Was not that the Law? Anna, lowly as she was, grasped a great truth when she assured him that "to forgive is what we're here for, if folks could only get it in their heads," and her prayer was no other than beautiful when she prayed:

"I hope all of us will have the grace to forgive if it ever comes our turn."

Père Monnier had preached to himself as well as to

his parishioners; he had been admonished by the lowly; his turn had come. Was he to have the grace for which Anna prayed?

As the parishioners went their ways home they gathered in groups to talk of the sermon that had come to them with a power never before felt.

"I know what was at the bottom of that," said Buttons, as he opened the post-office door to distribute the weekly mail and to accommodate his neighbors with groceries. "Genevieve was in his mind. Of that I'm as sure as where I be standing. He misses her, I'll warrant, and you see he has been a bit harsh, so he takes it to himself, and why shouldn't he? If he don't forgive and forget, a man of his cloth and goodness, how do you expect poor sinners like Buttons and the likes of him to set the lesson? Of course, I know as well as any of you that she didn't do right, and for the wrong I'm old enough to know that she'll suffer as long as she lives—suffering enough, poor thing! But the waters that have passed turn no mills. The deed is done; the child is God knows where! In my day I have guided too many fellows like the one she went away with to have a high opinion of her comfort. But that's not the question, as far as I can get it through my head; the question is just this, and I reckon I ain't out of my depths either: Ain't she the lost sheep? and ain't it the Père's duty to look her up? and ain't it our duty to be glad if she's getting along nicely, and if she's not to welcome her home? I'm for taking up a subscription and giving it to Père Monnier, just saying: 'We know you give away too much to have anything, and seeing that you have been sick, and thinking that a little rest would do you a world of good, and knowing if you stay here you won't take any rest, the folks put this little present in your hand to take with it a bit of vacation.' How's that?"

There was a murmur of assent until William Cagy spoke.

"You won't catch the Père that way, I fear," said Cagy. "He'll play his old capers on you. He'll take the purse, but he'll donate it to the church, and he'll remain where he is, working and working until there is nothing left of him. But if you want to heed Buttons, count me in for my share of the reckoning. There's no man I owe more to, and there's no man I would give as much to. It's himself that never put his heart in a dollar. The man in his parish who begrudges him a dollar hasn't a heart the size of a fly."

While this discussion was going on in the post-office, Napoleon, also full of the sermon that had begot such talk, was anxious to engage Anna on its merits. Coming from the church, as was his wont, with his dogs barking at his heels, and finding Anna removing her bonnet and shawl preparatory to putting on her calico apron and testing the singing roast in the oven, he shouted, "That took me, Anna;" to which Anna, with fire in her eye for the dogs that were bringing dust on their huge paws to soil her well-mopped floor, replied:

"There's always something taking you somewhere or another. I never saw you yet that you were not complaining. You're a queer soldier, you are, in my eyes. It's a wonder the war didn't scare you into a fit or something like it. I wish something would take your dogs. Just look at the way they're nosing around, ready to toss pans and pots! My heart's broke with you and your dogs, Mr. Napoleon. I cannot leave this kitchen long enough to take off my bonnet and shawl. If I do it is farewell to the roast! These dogs of yours have the ways of the bad man. They can open that oven there, Mr. Napoleon, with their noses as well as better-gifted folk with their hands, and once it's opened, you won't shut it again for anything that's left in it. Their noses are so tempered now with stealing that a hot coal wouldn't disturb the thieves. If you had to cook for the brutes you wouldn't be in such conceit with them, but you have only the play."

Napoleon, for the first time in his life, did not seem to mind her raillery. He dropped into an easy-chair, lifted the saucy cat, muttering: "My! what a tongue, Anna! Where I was soldiering they would not let it wag an hour. Why don't you understand folks before you commence your tongue-thrashing? I don't pay much attention to dogs or anything else these times. I have a bigger bother on my brain, I can tell you. But a man can't open his mouth lately around here, the Père's saying nothing and you're scolding. I was going to talk about the sermon when your alarm went off, and no call for it, for it wasn't the right time."

"The sermon," said Anna, "the sermon. I had two handkerchers, and they're like dishcloths; yes, they be. That tells where his words went. I never heard him swing his words the way he did to-day; did you, Napoleon? I was thinking it hit himself if it hit anybody; mind how his tears bubbled with all his working to keep them down. They just shot right through the skin and came tumbling down his face, just as natural as you please. I know who's our lost sheep and his, too. I couldn't help, when he was talking so much of Bergeron's girl, to give him a shot about something nearer home, and I'm judging by his talk he took it. I don't see how he can rest easy and Genevieve God only knows where. Is everybody to be forgiven but her? If I could only know where she is I would go myself. I have a bit of money for two. I wouldn't eat up much of it myself."

"Don't talk too much, Anna. You know what

was done for V., and you know too what she did; so if he forgives, it won't be himself but the Lord that will do it. Yes, it runs against the grain to have any one belonging to us do as V. did. I want her as much as you do, but I don't want him blamed for her doing."

"Who's blaming?" shouted Anna indignantly. "You had aye a queer way for twisting folks' talk, and you don't seem to have mended. I didn't blame anybody. I would do as much for the Père as you or anybody else, and that's not saying either that I can't have my say too about the poor, motherless child. Out of sight, out of mind, with you, Mr. Napoleon."

"Anna," said Napoleon, looking disgusted, "what else can I expect from you, a woman that has never travelled? Your flow of speech has neither rhyme nor reason. I guess I'll leave you to vent your spite on the cat. After you get the dinner off your mind you'll be a bit more comfortable."

As he left the kitchen he heard his name called, and turning in the direction of the sound saw to his delight Ruth O'Connor and one he took to be her husband standing on the church steps viewing the well-shaven lawn.

"Come here, Napoleon," said Ruth, "and shake my husband's hand. He knows all about you. We drove here, and luckily just came in time for the sermon. I was glad that Mr. O'Connor had the chance of hearing Père Monnier. It will explain to him in some way our loyalty to the Père. I saw you and dear old Anna in the church, but I could not get my eyes on Genevieve. Perhaps she has so changed that I would not know her on first sight. The place looks familiar, and my husband is charmed with the woods and lakes of the North. It is his first trip to the Adirondacks, and like every traveller that visits them once he vows that this trip will not be the last. So you see I will not be such a stranger as I have been."

"Why didn't you come into the house," said Napoleon, "instead of staying here? for dine with us you must, mind; none of your excuses. It's not often you come. I thought I would never put my eyes on you. Says I, once she's married and settled down, that ends her travelling; she'll have to forget the country and take to the bricks."

"How could you say that, Napoleon? I could never forget my home and the green graves that you have so dutifully attended. Ruth may not just write as often as she ought, but her heart loves the Northland. I have too many interests here, too many to forget. There's no change to you. Just the same old, laughing, fun-making Napoleon that used to bother me and Genevieve."

There were tears in Napoleon's eyes as he led the

O'Connors to the little dining-room where Père Monnier sat sipping his morning coffee.

After the long and hearty greeting, and when the questions regarding health were passed, the little party retired to the library so full of memories to Ruth.

"There are not many changes here, Mrs. O'Connor; a few more old books, that's all," said Père Monnier as he presented chairs to his guests.

"I miss Genevieve," said Ruth, conscious that something must have happened to her, or else her voice and footstep would have been heard. "I thought she would have been the first to greet me. Is she sick—gone away? What has become of her? I had Mr. O'Connor's ears filled with her praise. He is very anxious to see his wife's favorite pupil."

"Genevieve is not here, Ruth," responded the Père. "She, foolish girl, has run off and married, and since then I have not heard a word from her, although I am more than anxious to have some news. It has been a great blow, so much so that I have not mentioned her name in the house since she left. You know better than any stranger may know the care with which she was brought up, and then to turn round and run off with a young man of whom we know practically nothing has been to us cause of great sorrow. We must, as I said to-day, all forgive. I forgive Genevieve, and I pray that her life will be well lived."

"Who was the lucky man?" asked Mrs. O'Connor, "and where were they married? This news staggers me. If it did not come from your own mouth I could not believe it—it's so strange."

"Well, Ruth, our story is short, and only hearsay at that. I will tell you all I know, and that is not very much. It seems that at one of our picnics Genevieve met the young man, whose name, if I remember aright, was James Dade Fortune, from your city. He called here a few times without my sanction or knowledge, and, to cut the story still shorter, ended his visits by eloping with Genevieve. We heard that they went to New York; but whether or not they did I have not the slightest knowledge. That is all the news. It often occurred to me that I ought to write to you and ask you to make some inquiries about Genevieve. You see our minds are not satisfied as to her happiness. She was so young and so wanting in experience, and the young man bore such a bad name, that as the days pass I am becoming more anxious."

"If he is anything to the Fortunes that I know," said Mr. O'Connor, "and his name assures me that he is, you have, Père, every reason to be anxious. The family is a miserable one, at least from my point of view."

"My husband is an out-and-out Socialist," interrupted Ruth.

"My wife exaggerates. I do not just call myself a Socialist, Père, but I should like to have a few reforms. This boy's father—I know it must be he—came to New York from Ireland a pauper. In those days he was all Irish, ranting about the 'Old Land' on every street-corner. He was to organize a company, march on England, free Ireland, and do a thousand feats beyond the wizards of old. I remember him once before a crowded hall, after two hours of continuous rant how dear Erin should be free, bringing down the house with: 'Paralyzed be my tongue if it defend not my land's fame; paralyzed be my hands if they defend not her glory!' He learned early in life that his race was gullible and blarney-loving, and he made it a point to give them as much as they could agreeably take, which, I assure your reverence, was quite a considerable quantity. His dupes, spell-bound, went up and down the community singing loud and long his praises. According to their chorus James Fortune was an unparalleled business man, a majestic orator, and ever so many more adjectives. When election came along he had not to ask for votes, his friends did the asking and the proffering, and just to oblige them he took the office, and made it pay well and be a step to a better one that soon came in his way. To be lucky in politics in our city means to be lucky in cash, for these things run together. Well, he played the Irish as long as he had a political ambition and wanted cash. When the day came that these things were no longer needed he became Scotch-Irish, laughed at his countrymen's folly, and as judge sat upon all their peculiarities. War with England, of which he talked so glibly in the days of his poverty, was now one of the follies of his youth that he desired forgotten. Sir William Drake, during his Washington winters, had taught him the absurdities of his youthful speeches. He did not tell the baronet, you may be sure, that had it not been for his 'youthful follies in speeches' he would never have had the honor of Sir William's acquaintance. I had the opportunity to show Fortune's countrymen his real character. It was a bit late, for then he had made his money out of them, and was, as he said, independent. I cut him up in *The Lookout*. Sarcasm and satire, judiciously mingled, were too much for him. Seeing his threats and bullyings were of no avail he tried to buy me off, but that was only a recommendation for more lashings. My score with him is a long one."

"I am afraid, Père, that my husband will tire you on the Fortune affair. It's his weak point, and I don't blame him."

"Continue," said Père Monnier. "Mr. O'Connor interests me very much. In my own ministry, in this country, I have seen again and again similar occurrences. My heart has bled for the poor led by such demagogues. If the past could only teach! but they will not give it a chance."

"I will tell you, then, since I have the Père's permission," continued O'Connor, "and my wife must not break in with modifying expressions as is her custom. My score is this: Years ago a woman lived in Fortune's house. The house belonged formerly to her parents, but Fortune added it to his estate by means known only to himself. No sooner was the breath out of the woman—I should have said she was dying with consumption—than her body was carted off to potter's field, and her child, who was left with an old washwoman, the only friend the dying woman had, driven into the street on a bitter night.

"I often told my wife how beautiful that child was. It is a good while since I bounced her on my knee, but I was so much interested in her that I believe I would know her anywhere. I was very poor in those days, but what I had I gave in a way that I will never be able to duplicate. My golden-headed little lass! often in these years I have thought of her. Yet her case is one of the many in our city. We are eloquent on the poverty and tyranny of Europe; we never stop to consider our own. If we did, as we must some day, for the cancer steadily grows, I believe there will be smash and revolution. Men shout of the great mass of common-sense we have that will quickly balance any ebullition. I tell you when poverty will have to show itself not in the alleys, but in our streets, your common-sense will have little show."

"What became of the child?" asked the Père, shifting uneasily his chair.

"That is difficult to say, Père. I had but one dollar between me and starvation. Luckily my room was paid for, so I gave the child the dollar, and to her guardian, old Sal, a poor creature, but as warm-hearted a one as ever breathed, the key of the room, telling them to be comfortable. Old Sal was mortally afraid of her husband, a broken-down, worthless fellow, that has since given her peace by departing for better or worse, I don't know which, and Sal, having no way to keep the child, gave her to an Italian showman who went out in the country somewhere. The Italian never returned to New York, for a cousin of his, who keeps a corner fruit-stand in New York, told me so. Italians congregate in one quarter, so it is easy for their friends to know when they come to town."

"You don't remember the Italian's name?" asked Père Monnier.

"I know it is the same name as that of his cousin, which is Parenti," continued O'Connor. "I am sure of it. So is my wife, as she markets enough with him to remember that much Italian."

"I remember the name," replied Ruth. "My

husband has given it correctly, but he is the lost man's nephew, not his cousin—a slight difference."

O'Connor laughed at the humor of his wife, and she gave him smile for smile.

"I fear I am too inquisitive," said Père Monnier, "but men in my business grow into bad practices. Let me ask another question, and then I will rest my cross-examination."

"Don't mind asking questions, Père, regarding the lost girl. It is one of my husband's weaknesses," said Mrs. O'Connor. "Charlie has, on that subject, begot essays, short stories, and no end of poetry. The lost child is an idealized memory, the contemplation of which fills his mind with wrath against society, but, as I tell him, these things are common and will, as you said to-day, last as long as selfishness reigns in place of sacrifice. Wherever you find such misery, you will also find that it arises from many causes. But I see you are impatient of a woman philosopher, so I will give way for your question."

"You could hold the floor, Ruth," said Père Monnier. "I am sure I would gladly listen to your comments on Mr. O'Connor's idealizing. My own question was this: Does Mr. O'Connor remember the child's name? I may as well confess that I am a little interested in this subject as well as your husband."

"Oh, yes, Père, I remember the child's name very well," replied Mr. O'Connor. "That I could not forget. Genevieve Bain they called her—at least that's what old Sal told me her name was, and she has a right to know, as, if I am not mistaken, she once said that she knew several of the child's people in Ireland. In fact I know she told me so."

"While you two discuss the lost," said Mrs. O'Connor, "I'll visit with Napoleon and Anna. Come, Napoleon, the kitchen will be our fort."

As soon as they had passed from the library Père Monnier, under the pretence of showing Mr. O'Connor a picture of Ruth taken years ago, put the photograph cabinet in his hand and retired to the church for a few minutes. On his return he discovered Mr. O'Connor with Genevieve's picture in his hand.

"You have found Genevieve's picture, Mr. O'Connor?"

"And more, Père, if I am in my senses, and I think I am, I have found the lost one. I cannot be mistaken. There are changes, as we should expect, but that is the face of Genevieve Bain. I know it is the more I look at it. These Fortunes do not stop at the first generation. You will see that child crushed by them as was her mother. I did not wish to say so before my wife, but I know it to be a fact that Fortune's oldest boy has been married. My God! the whole thing is sickening! I feel it all; I fear it all! Perhaps my wife was right the other night when she insisted that we passed Genevieve on the street, near Fifth Avenue. She was so sure of it that nothing would do her but we must follow. Whether Genevieve or not, whoever it was, it did not take her long to get out of our way. Surely this beats fiction!"

O'Connor held down his head as if in deep meditation.

"I believe," said Père Monnier, running his long fingers through his hair, "that your surmises are true, but I will ask as a favor that, outside of Ruth, they be held secret."

"Not even Ruth shall know them, Père. It would do no good; it might only dislodge the Genevieve that she loves."

"Thank you, Mr. O'Connor." And Père Monnier's sentence was left unfinished, owing to the return of Ruth, leading old Anna to shake hands with her husband.

"You are done with the lost one," said Ruth.

"Done!" exclaimed O'Connor.

"We are going to dine or lunch, whatever you call it," said the Père. "It is about time. Anna, can't you give your friends the best? I fear that will be poor enough."

"We must go off at once," said Mrs. O'Connor. "I promised to dine with Mr. Dixon, my father's old partner."

"And I must follow my wife," said O'Connor,

laughing. "I fear otherwise I might be lost. I told the driver to be here on time. Here he comes. This trip will soon be repeated. To see your mountains once is to long ever after to visit them."

"Well, I will not ask you to stay, because you owe no man more than Mr. Dixon," said the Père, rising to lead the way. "But you must come soon again and stay longer. I have only just broken the ice with your husband."

As the carriage drove away O'Connor shouted with his farewell: "You will soon hear from me."

Père Monnier bowed, and, turning to Napoleon, said:

"I want to catch the New York night train. Have me there in time. And while I am away let Anna get Genevieve's room just as she left it. I want a few days' vacation. When I return you will know all."

Napoleon's eyes were wet as he stammered: "Everything just as you wish."

CHAPTER XIII.

MORS JANUA VITÆ.

"WE'VE surely had sleep enough," said old Sal, as she jumped from the bed and pulled up the curtain. "It must be near noon. Why, Genevieve, you're awake! I was going to let you sleep, but you'll be just as well up. You'll sleep better for it to-night. Sleeping and eating and grinding the music-box take all my time. You were terribly restless last night, tossing and turning all the time. I thought you were either sick or dreaming. You gave out a flow of talk that would do credit to a lawyer."

"Did I talk, Sal?" asked Genevieve, rising and dressing. "I never heard that I was guilty of that charge before."

"Did you talk? you did more than talk; you screamed and took on as if you were going to be killed. I think you were feverish awhile. It looked like it, anyway. What kind of dreams had you? Nightmares, I'll venture. I used to have an odd one of them when I was young."

"No, Sal; I guess it was real old-fashioned dreaming I was at—dreaming about home."

"Yes, you are right there, Genevieve. Folks will dream about home; no mistake of that. I lie down some nights, and I hardly touch the pillow than I'm over in Ireland with a lot of other girls that are all dead and gone. It does beat anything how their faces and actions, just as natural as life, will come in a dream. But if you wanted them when you're awake they wouldn't come near you—no, they wouldn't."

"I was excited last night, Sal. I suppose it was my imagination that was playing me a trick. When I was going last night to meet you, I thought I saw in advance of me the man that brought me up, and the quicker I walked, and the nearer I came, the resemblance became the more striking. He turned into the Cathedral, but I was so afraid that I thought my heart could be heard by everybody passing; I was unable to follow him. I stood on the street like a block of stone. It might have been my imagination. Whatever it was, it set me agoing all night."

"You don't look the picture of health, dear." And old Sal drew the girl's head to her breast. "Your eyes are full of tears, and my eye is quick enough to see sorrow in your face. You're worrying about work, and that's foolish, for just as soon as the O'Connors return you'll get something, and until they come you're as welcome here as the sunlight, that you are, dear, and you must think that way. As

I told you, I have not much, but what I have you're welcome to, and I give thanks that it is enough, anyway, to keep us in shelter and from being hungry. And again it's something, poor as it is, that's lasting. No need, Genevieve, of crying or worrying. As my man used to say, ' Every lane has a turn if we follow it long enough.' He died before his turned, but that's not saying it will be the same with everybody else. Your turn will come just as quick as I see Charlie O'Connor. He has a great head on him, and he'll take to you at once, that I know he will."

"I hope some one will take to me, for I am pretty desolate, Sal," said Genevieve, flooding the woman's face with tears. "I have been a terrible girl. I deserve all the punishment I must suffer. You will not be angry with me, Sal? You won't put me away because I tell you this?"

"God bless your wit, child, what would Sal put you away for? Haven't we all been bad and foolish? It's only the mercy of God we're living at all. As one of the salvation women said to me last night, 'Sal, we're all sinners, but we can be washed.' Put you out! No, dear; I had never that name. You won't leave here as long as I have a crust. I don't think I was so happy since I was a girl as I have been these few days listening to you. Your mind is full of everything. Says I to myself, last night when I was grinding out a waltz, 'Genevieve was brought up in the lap of luxury and educated high.' I just come to my opinion by your talk and the way you sing. It's not the brought-up poor folks that can use your words and trill your voice; it's the gentry. Then I had only to ask you once to sing. If it took coaxing it was a sure sign that you come from poor folks. They would have to put on airs and make fools of themselves. You're smiling, child, in your tears at my queer way of judging folks; but I bet I'm right. Long lessons in any school will make you know something in the long run. The first time you spoke, I knew you were no street-walker. God between them and me and harm, that I did, dear; and I was not afraid to give you a place and a bite. Don't cry; all will be well as soon as Charlie comes, and you're well enough until he does come."

"Oh, yes; I am well enough—better than I ought to be, Sal. But I'm breaking my heart for a glimpse of home," said Genevieve, throwing her arms around the woman's neck and sobbing loudly.

"I don't blame you a bit," said Sal, mingling her tears with those of Genevieve. "There's no place like home, no matter how poor it is. I wish I never had left mine. It's many the cup of sorrow I've drunk since I sailed on the *Blackbird*. Poor as it was, too, I never found its equal since I left it. Yes, my dear, I don't wonder at your grief; and I was just thinking that maybe it was the man that brought you

up that's lonesome for you and has come on to look
you up. That would be no way strange. What
kind of a looking man was he?"

As Sal spoke there was a loud knocking on the
door, that made the women hastily rise to their feet.

"I wonder who is coming to give us a call, Genevieve," said Sal, as she drew the door-bolt and
cautiously opened the door. "Wouldn't it be luck
if it was one of the O'Connors? It sounds like
Charlie's rap. If it is, let me do the talking."

Genevieve, standing against the bedpost, shook
her head in assent, and with her hands brushed back
her wayward hair, and arranged, as best she could,
her faded skirt.

If this was the O'Connors, how could she meet
them? What would Ruth think? Would not old
Sal, who had been so kind to her, brand her as a
hypocrite when Ruth would speak of their long years
of friendship? She prayed for strength and waited
their coming.

"Good-morning, your reverence," said Sal, as a
tall figure in clerical dress entered. "You're the
first of your cloth to darken my door; but it's no lie
to say that you're a hundred thousand times welcome.
It always does me good to see one of ye, whether you
speak to me or not. I had priests in my family in
the old country; indeed I had, and their likes couldn't
be found in the whole county. Come in and rest a

bit. I'm ashamed I haven't a better home, but beggars cannot be choosers. I shouldn't grumble, but thank God. There are thousands worse off this good morning."

"Why, I could be as happy as a king in this cosey nook," said the stranger.

Genevieve, at the sound of Sal's voice, had turned her back on the door, hardly knowing why, perhaps from shame. At the sound of the stranger's voice, unconsciously she wheeled around and faced him. One glance, and the trembling, sobbing girl fell on her knees.

Before Père Monnier had time to speak, Genevieve, her eyes asking his eyes for a sign of forgiveness, had begun her confession.

"Father, forgive me, for I have sinned, and through my fault. For all your kindness I have given you but ingratitude. I have brought sorrow to your house. I was young—I was heedless—I was foolish. I had seen but your life, and I thought all men were as noble and as good as you are. Ah, now I know there are few Père Monniers! Oh! if I could hope that you would forgive me—that you would let me see Napoleon and Anna, and my home, if it was only for a minute, I would do whatever you would say—I would go wherever you would send me, and never complain. I loved him—loved him down in my heart. For hours and hours he told me how he loved me—that he would die if I did not give him love; and I gave him love—my heart; and he took it and drove a dagger through it, befouled it, blackened it, killed it! O Père—O Père! It was not a man but a serpent I was pitted against! After a mock marriage before a justice—I knew then I was doing wrong, but, having fled, I dreaded to return; I was weak—he took me to New York, tired of me in a few weeks, fled from me, leaving a note saying he was a married man, and hoping that I should forgive and forget his villany. He valued woman's honor so light. I left the hotel, took the cheapest lodging I could find, sought work. Nobody wanted me at any price. When my money was gone, I went out on the street, asking God to forgive and take care of me, His lost lamb, and He guided me to Sal, here, and through Him she took compassion on me. I am lonely—so lonely! I want to go home. Can't I go home and be your little girl again? Do not say no; have pity on Genevieve!"

Père Monnier's eyes glanced from the weeping girl to the rough brass crucifix which hung on the bedpost. Genevieve, noticing this, turned her eyes to the same object.

As both their eyes rested on Sal's only Irish keepsake—a keepsake that had comforted her in all her sorrows, making hope spring from even her greatest miseries—Genevieve clasped it, pulled it from the pin which held it, and pointing with it to Père Monnier, in childish voice cried, "*He* would forgive me!"

"And I," said Père Monnier, the bitter tears running down his cheeks, "forgive you for His sake."

At his words Genevieve fell forward in a swoon.

Père Monnier, bending over her, lifted her up tenderly and laid her on the bed.

In a few minutes she revived, stretched her hand to him as he sat by her bedside, and then, like a worn-out child, fell softly asleep. Père Monnier's heart deeply ached as he compared the pale, emaciated, sleeping girl with the laughing, gay-hearted maiden that was wont to decorate his writing-desk with sweet-smelling flowers.

Old Sal, who had witnessed the strange scene without in any way interfering, now stole up to the bed and gazed long and strangely on the face of Genevieve.

"I must thank you for the interest you have taken in this poor child. Her life," and Père Monnier sorrowfully cast his keen eyes on Genevieve's face, "has been ruined by a scoundrel. How sick she looks! If I am not mistaken, our Genevieve will not trouble us long. To have found her, even as she is, lifts a heavy load from my heart. They will hardly know her at home. What sorrow will come to the hearts of Napoleon and Anna! She was their treasure. And to think that in such a short space of time the blood should leave her face, and the light they loved grow dim in her eyes! Too early in life has she been smote with the sword of sorrow. I know the wound is fatal."

"Poor child!" muttered Sal, bending over and kissing the sleeping girl. "She's too young indeed to be made the prey of a villain, but she's just the age when villains can best decoy, and under the cloak of love bring ruin. Love may be all right, but it has ruined more than it has blessed."

"That is not love," said the Père.

"But those that it ruins think it is, and only know different when the ruin comes," spoke Sal rather tartly, as she again bent and kissed Genevieve, picking up from the quilt the brass crucifix that had fallen from the sleeping girl's hand. Putting her treasured keepsake in its usual place on the bedpost, with a strange look in her eyes, the woman continued:

"Aye, your reverence, and it's the people who pretend to be *His* people" (pointing to the crucifix) "that do the ruin. They speak fine words, they go to church, but their voice is a mockery, and their hearts are rotten! What they preach with their mouths they belie by their hearts. They will bring Christ to everybody far away. At home they try with all their might to banish Him from our lives. They can quote you texts of the Bible, but they never put them into practice. They look on the poor as grease—that's what Charlie O'Connor told me long ago—grease to run their machinery. It hurts them to think that the poor have souls. I don't believe some of them think we have. Anyway they don't act like it. I remember when I was young hearing Mass on an Irish hill-side—we had no chapel then; the priest (may God be good to him! he lived from hand to mouth just like the rest of us, and not half so proud, though he studied in Spain, and was full of learning from the crown of his head to the sole of his foot) said that all Christians would be judged by two rules. One was if they loved God; the other if they loved their neighbors.

"Aye, that's the tape-line to put on them. Measure them by it and what will you find but hypocrites, pharisees? They speak the law, but they don't live up to it, do they? Their god is themselves. Love their neighbors! They may if they happen to be rich and in their set. They claim the right of saying who is their neighbor. Would any one of them claim me as their sister, or give me a word of courage?"

The old woman broke out in harsh laughter and continued: "I guess not, your reverence; they think more of their dogs. Poverty is a crime, and it is treated as a crime. We talk of being free here and treated equally. None but fools babble that. Treated equally when two-thirds of us are slaves—grease for the grinding-machinery of the other third!

Heavens! what fine yarns are spun to make us carry our loads! 'People get tired of the best tunes,' says Charlie, and this tune of freedom, played to a lot of slaves, has about had its day. The slaves have found out it was only sarcasm. These fine Christians, with their texts about the 'blessedness of poverty,' while they steal our substance and grind out our lives to pay for their vanities, have nearly come to the end of their rope. We don't want texts explained by hypocrites—no, we don't! They know too well how to twist them into ropes for our binding. You know what they say over in Ireland if you put your foot too tight down upon a worm; small and poor and dirty as it is, it will turn its head at you and squirm, which is its way of fighting. Patience a bit, and if you live you'll see what's coming, and I'll dance a jig when it comes. I tell you I smell it every night on Fifth Avenue. *It's smash and revolution! and it's coming because rich people won't keep the law!* Charlie O'Connor said years ago it was bound to come; but now I know it is! As I told you, I smell it on the street. Charlie, he's a great scholar, says: 'Sal, mind what I told you. I see it coming—in newspapers every morning—in magazines—in books. It *creeps;* but when it gets here things will be lively.' I think that your reverence—a man of your cloth, whose duty is to be as Christ was among the poor—should hear, now and then, a bit of the rumble. If you lived in this city, unless you wanted to be deaf, you would hear it from the mouths of the toilers—from the pressed-dry children—from all those that would like to follow Christ if they had a chance. Don't get afraid of my talk. I'm bitter, no doubt of that, but there are thousands just as bitter. Perhaps they have more sense, so they manage to keep in; but when the smash comes they'll be out with their hammers and hit the hardest blows. Charlie says you don't find volcanoes on the surface."

Old Sal for the third time bent down and pressed the sleeping girl's head to her breast.

Père Monnier's quick eye noticed that the harshness which crept into the woman's face while preaching her doctrine of revolution faded away into kindliness as she touched Genevieve.

Nor was he astonished to find in the mouth of one so lowly such strange utterances. History had taught him, and years amid the poor had confirmed history's teaching, that all revolutions spring from the discontent of the toilers. When their sufferings become unbearable all that is needed is a leader to change their patience into defiance. Another truth well known to him was that those who gave the cause for revolutions heeded no warnings until the demoniac fury of the revolutionists told them that from those to whom no mercy has been shown, in the day of their might no mercy need be expected.

Old Sal's talk had more and more convinced Père Monnier, if such a thing were possible, of the soundness of what years of study of men and books had taught him, that the world was drifting away from Christ and losing His Gospel—a loss which was accountable for the utterances of Sal, and for all the misery and sorrow which begot such utterances. Love, as taught by Christ, had once conquered the world; but pagan selfishness had again unfurled her banner, unsheathed her sword, and counted thousands beneath her tempting standard. What was wanted, to his mind, was a constant teaching of the very fundamentals of religion. Apostles imbued with the spirit of Christ, as fearless as St. Paul, to preach, to rich and poor alike, honesty and charity, to make clear to their minds that the Gospel of Christ is not merely to be read but to be lived.

If this truth could be made so manifest that men would hearken to it, then would harmony and peace enter the modern world. All other remedies preached were vain—the spawn of blind, man-made philosophy. Love alone could conquer the world, but Christ must tend love's fire. Would men hearken to the Gospel and be saved, or must smash and revolution, for which old Sal so fervently prayed, come before the scales should fall from their eyes and sanity rule in their minds?

Père Monnier, prayerful and man-loving, held that

the vineyard was ripe if the apostles were ready. In his own limited sphere he had proved this. He loved that saying of St. Paul:

"Christ died for us: much more therefore, being now justified by His blood, shall we be saved from wrath through Him."

His thoughts—thoughts that first awoke in his mountain home—were banished for awhile by Sal's importuning him to forgive "the child," and his reward would be great. "She's at best," said the woman, "but a bit of a child, born and bred in hardships until you got her, and my curse on the man that led her back into hardship!"

Sal paused for a moment as if in thought, and then continued: "It's in the blood, but I do not know from which side she could have taken it. A scoundrel played her mother the same game. Her grandmother was the cream of the land, and her mother as fine a girl as you could pick in New York. Aye, it's true. I saw her when there was no beauty in her: not a speck after sickness and sorrow had made her a skeleton, a poor-looking one at that. What strange things will happen! Here's her poor little child that Fortune, after robbing the mother, threw in the street. Genevieve," and Sal printed a kiss on her girl's head, "I little thought that you and I should meet again, and in the very room you went out of long ago. I thought you were dead and, like your mother, at rest, but there you lie with the thing that killed your mother in your face. I see it as I saw it in hers. Aye, there you lie—Charlie O'Connor's golden-headed lass."

The fire and fierceness had fled from Sal's speech; her voice was low and tender; the real Sal, the Sal that had divided her bread with the homeless James Fortune was now speaking, and the Père was not slow to discern the coming of the woman's better nature.

"Of course, Sal, I shall forgive her," said Père Monnier. "If I would not forgive, how could I teach others to forgive? After her sleep she will be strong enough to travel home. By to-morrow morning we shall be in my little parish where everybody loves our Genevieve. Anna's care and Napoleon's jokes, and the good things Billy Buttons and Cagy will find for her in the woods, and the dainties that everybody will bring, must recruit her, if that be possible. I know she wants to go home at once. I could not bear to put her in a hospital and leave her. Our child has seen too much of the stranger. From your talk I take it for granted that you know all about the child. I know but little. She had been travelling with an Italian showman, beating a drum, doing little tricks, and taking up the pennies of the bystanders. Her master died in my parish, and as I happened to be driving along at the time, I took the child as a companion for my old housekeeper. We educated her, brought her up as best we could. She was the pet of our household. Yes; a charming girl was Genevieve, amiable and obedient. You have already heard her story—how a ruffian decoyed her, blasted her young life. If a Fortune robbed her mother, as you say, of her personal goods, it was a Fortune that robbed Genevieve of her honor, which is much more precious. Yes!" and the fire flashed in the Père's eyes, and a strong man trembled, " the ruffian's name was James Dade Fortune. His father, who lives on Fifth Avenue and calls himself the Hon. James Fortune, has sent his scamp to Europe and laughs at this poor girl's plight. But the arm of the Lord is long, and vengeance is His, and I know His vengeance will follow, by land and sea."

Père Monnier sat down on the edge of the bed, cast a look at the broken bit of clay, once the treasure of his household, bowed his head, and wept.

The dreams he had woven around Genevieve, the ideals he had conjured—all, all, were fled.

To build in the future, to dream, to conjure up ideals, was but vanity of vanities—a boyish trick of blowing soap-bubbles. Act well the day; no man knows whereof the morrow. A few short weeks ago the sleeping girl was full of life; warm, red blood rushing through her veins, fresh and rosy, full of laughter and mirth. To-day life was on the wane; the blood stagnant; freshness faded, rosiness gone;

sorrow pressing life's juice from her mangled heart.

He would bear her back to his mountain home, teach her, more and more, the love of the Master whose servant he was, until she, too, would understand that better is the day of death than the day of one's birth. His text-books would be love and sorrow.

Old Sal, who had listened patiently to the Père's recital, as soon as he had sat down and bowed his head broke into a diatribe against the Fortunes and the necessity of smash and revolution.

"*I* cannot see," screeched the old woman, "how God permits one family to do so much to another family as the Fortunes have done to that child and her mother. Is there such a thing as justice anyway? I sometimes doubt it. Scoundrels possess the fat of the land; the good people but poverty. Yes; we want smash to equalize it a bit."

Her words awoke the dreaming Père.

"Don't speak in that way, Sal. There is justice, but it may not be meted out always on this side of life. Yet justice there will be. From smash and revolution it can never come."

His words quelled the woman's fierceness and turned her thoughts from the Fortunes to Genevieve.

"Forgive me, your reverence," she said. "I am an ignorant woman, and often don't just express myself well; but with all that I know about the Fortunes and this child it's hard to keep my temper. Yes; you are right. There must be justice somewhere; but to my old head it seems too long until after death to wait for it. If I had your head I could see it better. I don't get anything from books. Just what I see—misery all around me, and then I think on it all, here alone. I don't take it to myself to be very smart or else I would have known that girl before to-day. As soon as she dropped on her knees and began to beg off I knew her at once. It was the same face and the same actions she used for me to keep her when I had to give her to Parenti. And so he's dead, and that's how you come to get her? Well; I knew him for years, and he was a kind, good man, else he would not have had Genevieve Bain. I could not keep her myself. I was too poor for that, and I have a terrible fear of these poorhouses—God keep me from darkening one of their doors! When I gave her to Parenti I done the best I could. When a body's poor they cannot do much. So you brought her up? I knew by her talk and ways that she had no common bringing up. Well, thanks be to God! when she needed a home I had one for her and a bit to eat. That I was able to do that will comfort me many a cold night on the avenue when pennies are scarce and the passing folk selfish."

The old woman sat down and cried bitterly.

Genevieve awoke, drew her hand over her eyes as

if to brush away the tear-mist, then, seeing Père Monnier, half arose and, stretching her arms like a child seeking a mother's breast, cried:

"Uncle, I want to go home!"

"We shall go, dear, at once," said the gentle, sweet voice of the Père. "Anna and Napoleon will be angry because we stayed away so long, and the dogs—what a noise they will make to welcome us! Yes; we must go home at once."

* * * * *

It was a beautiful day in early autumn. The trees were as yet untouched by that red which is at once beauty and decay. High up in their branches sat the robin with a bolder if less sweet note than he plays in the summer sunshine. He had reared his little family, which, filled with the wine of youth, made merry around him. His care was over, and he showed his gladness in his song. The little country parsonage looked cheery with its flower-beds and flowering shrubs. The many-colored asters were in full bloom. A stranger passing would surely seek such a nook to hide away from sorrow.

There was a strange bustle in the parsonage. Napoleon came from the house, entered the little church, prayed for awhile and then re-entered the house. A few minutes later Anna, hot tears coursing down her wrinkled face, followed his example. Then came the doctor, an old friend of Père Monnier, looking sad and worn from his vigils.

With his going was heard a voice floating out of the open window:

> *"Pax huic domini*
> *Et omnibus habitantibus in ea.*
> *Asperges me, Domine."*

Then the voice sank, becoming more like a long-drawn sigh than speech. It was the voice of Père Monnier anointing Genevieve, preparing her for the last journey that mortals make. Kneeling around her little bed, grief-broken and speechless, were Napoleon and Anna.

"You will feel better now," said the Père, as he finished the last ceremonies of his Church.

"Much better, uncle," whispered the dying girl. "Uncle, I know—I know *now* that the wages of sin is death."

"And you know, O child, that if your sins were as red as scarlet, He would make them as white as snow."

"I know He has done so, uncle. I am happy. I must leave you; but in a little while you will come to poor Genevieve, and Anna and Napoleon will come, and we shall all be together again. Raise me up, uncle. I want to see Anna and Napoleon once again. Raise me up that I may see the church, the flowers, and the blessed sunshine once more."

He raised her up, and through the open window

came the murmur of the river she loved, and the robin's song. The trees were green, the flowers fair, life and love were all around her, but the spirit of Genevieve would no longer tarry in its house of clay.

* * * * *

It has often been a cause of wonder why Père Monnier spent his life in the little mountain town. The readers of this story can now tell why. Genevieve's grave is there.

Benziger Brothers' New Plan for Disseminating Catholic Literature

A NEW PLAN FOR SECURING
Catholic Books on Easy Payments

Small Monthly Payments.   Books Delivered Immediately.
All New Copyright Works by the Foremost Writers

PRINTED FROM NEW PLATES, ON GOOD PAPER, SUBSTANTIALLY BOUND IN CLOTH

A MOST LIBERAL OFFER!

The following pages contain a list of the books in our Catholic Circulating Library which can be had from us on the easy-payment plan.

Though the books are sold on easy payments, the prices are lower than the regular advertised prices.

Any library advertised in these pages will be sent to you immediately on receipt of $1.00.

CATHOLIC CIRCULATING LIBRARY

THE PLAN FOR FORMING === READING CIRCLES ===

Dues only 10 Cents a Month

A New Book Every Month | Total Cost for a
$12 Worth of Books to Read | Year, $1.20

THIS EXPLAINS THE PLAN

You form a Reading Club, say of twelve members, and order one of the Libraries from us.

Each member pays you ten cents a month, and you remit us $1.00 a month, thus paying us for the books.

On receipt of the first dollar we will send you a complete library. You give each member a book. After a month all the members return their books to you and you give them another one. The books are exchanged in this way every month till the members have read the twelve volumes in the Library. After the twelfth month the books may be divided among the members (each getting one book to keep) or the books may be given to your Pastor for a parish library.

Then you can order from us a second library on the same terms as above. In this way you can keep up your Reading Circle from year to year at a trifling cost.

On the following pages will be found a list of the books in the different Libraries. They are the best that can be had.

MAIL A DOLLAR BILL TO-DAY AND ANY LIBRARY WILL BE FORWARDED AT ONCE

THE OTHER PLAN

Or if, instead of forming a Reading Circle, you wish to get a Library for yourself or your family, all you need do is to remit a dollar bill and any Library will be forwarded to you at once. Then you pay One Dollar a month.

BENZIGER BROTHERS

NEW YORK:
36-38 Barclay Street.

CINCINNATI:
343 Main Street.

CHICAGO:
211-213 Madison Street.

Catholic Circulating Library

Dues, 10c. a Month

2 New Books Every Month

JUVENILE BOOKS

20 Copyrighted Stories for the Young, by the Best Authors

Special net price, $10.00

You get the books at once, and have the use of them, while making easy payments

Read explanation of our Circulating Library plan on first page

Juvenile Library A

TOM PLAYFAIR; OR, MAKING A START. By Rev. F. J. Finn, S.J. "The best boy's book that ever came from the press."

THE CAVE BY THE BEECH FORK. By Rev. H. S. Spalding, S.J. "This is a story full of go and adventure."

HARRY RUSSELL, A ROCKLAND COLLEGE BOY. By Rev. J. E. Copus, S.J. "Father Copus takes the college hero where Father Finn has left him, through the years to graduation."

CHARLIE CHITTYWICK. By Rev. David Bearne, S.J. Father Bearne shows a wonderful knowledge and fine appreciation of boy character. There is no mark of mawkishness in the book.

NAN NOBODY. By Mary T. Waggaman. "Keeps one fascinated till the last page is reached."

LOYAL BLUE AND ROYAL SCARLET. By Marion A. Taggart. "Will help keep awake the strain of hero worship and ideal patriotism."

THE GOLDEN LILY. By Katharine T. Hinkson. "Another proof of the author's wonderful genius."

THE MYSTERIOUS DOORWAY. By Anna T. Sadlier. "A bright, sparkling book."

OLD CHARLMONT'S SEED-BED. By Sara T. Smith. "A delightful story of Southern school life."

THE MADCAP SET AT ST. ANNE'S. By Marion J. Brunowe. "Plenty of fun and frolic, with high moral principle."

BUNT AND BILL. By Clara Mulholland. "There are passages of true pathos and humor in this pretty tale."

THE FLOWER OF THE FLOCK. By Maurice F. Egan. "They are by no means faultless young people and their hearts lie in the right places."

PICKLE AND PEPPER. By Ella L. Dorsey. "This story is clever and witty—there is not a dull page."

A HOSTAGE OF WAR. By Mary G. Bonesteel. "A wide-awake story, brimful of incident and easy humor."

AN EVERY DAY GIRL. By Mary T. Crowley. "One of the few tales that will appeal to the heart of every girl."

AS TRUE AS GOLD. By Mary E. Mannix. "This book will make a name for itself."

AN HEIR OF DREAMS. By S. M. O'Malley. "The book is destined to become a true friend of our boys."

THE MYSTERY OF HORNBY HALL. By Anna T. Sadlier. Sure to stir the blood of every real boy and to delight with its finer touches the heart of every true girl."

TWO LITTLE GIRLS. By Lillian Mack. "A real tale of real children."

RIDINGDALE FLOWER SHOW. By Rev. David Bearne, S.J. "His sympathy with boyhood is so evident and his understanding so perfect."

20 Copyrighted Stories for the Young
By the Best Catholic Writers
SPECIAL NET PRICE, $10.00
$1.00 down, $1.00 a month

Read explanation of our Circulating Library plan on preceding pages

---

Juvenile Library B

HIS FIRST AND LAST APPEARANCE. By REV. F. J. FINN, S.J. Profusely illustrated. "A delightful story by Father Finn, which will be popular with the girls as well as with the boys."

THE SHERIFF OF THE BEECH FORK. By REV. H. S. SPALDING, S.J. "From the outset the reader's attention is captivated and never lags."

SAINT CUTHBERT'S. By REV. J. E. COPUS, S.J. "A truly inspiring tale, full of excitement."

THE TAMING OF POLLY. By ELLA LORAINE DORSEY. "Polly with her cool head, her pure heart and stern Western sense of justice."

STRONG-ARM OF AVALON. By MARY T. WAGGAMAN. "Takes hold of the interest and of the heart and never lets go."

JACK HILDRETH ON THE NILE. By C. MAY. "Courage, truth, honest dealing with friend and foe."

A KLONDIKE PICNIC. By ELEANOR C. DONNELLY. "Alive with the charm that belongs to childhood."

A COLLEGE BOY. By ANTHONY YORKE. "Healthy, full of life, full of incident."

THE GREAT CAPTAIN. By KATHARINE T. HINKSON. "Makes the most interesting and delightful reading."

THE YOUNG COLOR GUARD. By MARY G. BONESTEEL. "The attractiveness of the tale is enhanced by the realness that pervades it."

THE HALDEMAN CHILDREN. By MARY E. MANNIX. "Full of people entertaining, refined, and witty."

PAULINE ARCHER. By ANNA T. SADLIER. "Sure to captivate the hearts of all juvenile readers."

THE ARMORER OF SOLINGEN. By W. HERCHENBACH. "Cannot fail to inspire honest ambition."

THE INUNDATION. By CANON SCHMID. "Sure to please the young readers for whom it is intended."

THE BLISSYLVANIA POST-OFFICE. By MARION A. TAGGART. "Pleasing and captivating to young people."

DIMPLING'S SUCCESS. By CLARA MULHOLLAND. "Vivacious and natural and cannot fail to be a favorite."

BISTOURI. By A. MELANDRI. "How Bistouri traces out the plotters and foils them makes interesting reading."

FRED'S LITTLE DAUGHTER. By SARA T. SMITH. "The heroine wins her way into the heart of every one."

THE SEA-GULL'S ROCK. By J. SANDEAU. "The intrepidity of the little hero will appeal to every boy."

JUVENILE ROUND TABLE. FIRST SERIES. A collection of twenty stories by the foremost writers, with many full-page illustrations.

20 Copyrighted Stories for the Young
By the Best Catholic Writers
SPECIAL NET PRICE, $10.00
$1.00 down, $1.00 a month

Read explanation of our Circulating Library plan on preceding pages

---

Juvenile Library C

PERCY WYNN; OR, MAKING A BOY OF HIM. By REV. F. J. FINN, S.J. "The most successful Catholic juvenile published."

THE RACE FOR COPPER ISLAND. By REV. H. S. SPALDING, S.J. "Father Spalding's descriptions equal those of Cooper."

SHADOWS LIFTED. By REV. J. E. COPUS, S.J. "We know of no books more delightful and interesting."

HOW THEY WORKED THEIR WAY, AND OTHER STORIES. By MAURICE F. EGAN. "A choice collection of stories by one of the most popular writers."

WINNETOU, THE APACHE KNIGHT. By C. MAY. "Chapters of breathless interest."

MILLY AVELING. By SARA TRAINER SMITH. "The best story Sara Trainer Smith has ever written."

THE TRANSPLANTING OF TESSIE. By MARY T. WAGGAMAN. "An excellent girl's story."

THE PLAYWATER PLOT. By MARY T. WAGGAMAN. "How the plotters are captured and the boy rescued makes a very interesting story."

AN ADVENTURE WITH THE APACHES. By GABRIEL FERRY.

PANCHO AND PANCHITA. By MARY E. MANNIX. "Full of color and warmth of life in old Mexico."

RECRUIT TOMMY COLLINS. By MARY G. BONESTEEL. "Many a boyish heart will beat in envious admiration of little Tommy."

BY BRANSCOME RIVER. By MARION A. TAGGART. "A creditable book in every way."

THE QUEEN'S PAGE. By KATHARINE TYNAN HINKSON. "Will arouse the young to interest in historical matters and is a good story well told."

MARY TRACY'S FORTUNE. By ANNA T. SADLIER. "Sprightly, interesting and well written."

BOB-O'LINK. By MARY T. WAGGAMAN. "Every boy and girl will be delighted with Bob-o'Link."

THREE GIRLS AND ESPECIALLY ONE. By MARION A. TAGGART. "There is an exquisite charm in the telling."

WRONGFULLY ACCUSED. By W. HERCHENBACK. "A simple tale, entertainingly told."

THE CANARY BIRD. By CANON SCHMID. "The story is a fine one and will be enjoyed by boys and girls."

FIVE O'CLOCK STORIES. By S. H. C. J. "The children who are blessed with such stories have much to be thankful for."

JUVENILE ROUND TABLE. SECOND SERIES. A collection of twenty stories by the foremost writers, with many full-page illustrations.

20 Copyrighted Stories for the Young

By the Best Catholic Writers

SPECIAL NEW PRICE, $10.00

$1.00 down, $1.00 a month

Read explanation of our Circulating Library plan on preceding pages

Juvenile Library D

THE WITCH OF RIDINGDALE. By Rev. David Bearne, S.J. "Here is a story for boys that bids fair to equal any of Father Finn's successes."

THE MYSTERY OF CLEVERLY. By George Barton. There is a peculiar charm about this novel that the discriminating reader will ascribe to the author's own personality.

HARMONY FLATS. By C. S. Whitmore. The characters in this story are all drawn true to life, and the incidents are exciting.

WAYWARD WINIFRED. By Anna T. Sadlier. A story for girls. Its youthful readers will enjoy the vivid description, lively conversations, and plenty of striking incidents, all winding up happily.

TOM LOSELY: BOY. By Rev. J. E. Copus, S.J. Illustrated. The writer knows boys and boy nature, and small-boy nature too.

MORE FIVE O'CLOCK STORIES. By S. H. C. J. "The children who are blessed with such stories have much to be thankful for."

JACK O'LANTERN. By Mary T. Waggaman. This book is alive with interest. It is full of life and incident.

THE BERKLEYS. By Emma Howard Wight. A truly inspiring tale, full of excitement. There is not a dull page.

LITTLE MISSY. By Mary T. Waggaman. A charming story for children which will be enjoyed by older folk as well.

TOM'S LUCK-POT. By Mary T. Waggaman. Full of fun and charming incidents—a book that every boy should read.

CHILDREN OF CUPA. By Mary E. Mannix. One of the most thoroughly unique and charming books that has found its way to the reviewing desk in many a day.

FOR THE WHITE ROSE. By Katharine T. Hinkson. This book is something more than a story; but, as a mere story, it is admirably well written.

THE DOLLAR HUNT. From the French by E. G. Martin. Those who wish to get a *fascinating* tale should read this story.

THE VIOLIN MAKER. From the original of Otto v. Schaching, by Sara Trainer Smith. There is much truth in this simple little story.

"JACK." By S. H. C. J. As loving and lovable a little fellow as there is in the world is "Jack," the "pickle," the "ragamuffin," the defender of persecuted kittens and personal principles.

A SUMMER AT WOODVILLE. By Anna T. Sadlier. This is a beautiful book, in full sympathy with and delicately expressive of the author's creations.

DADDY DAN. By Mary T. Waggaman. This is a rattling good story for boys.

THE BELL FOUNDRY. By Otto v. Schaching. So interesting that the reader will find difficulty in tearing himself away.

TOORALLADDY. By Julia C. Walsh. An exciting story of the varied fortunes of an orphan boy from abject poverty in a dismal cellar to success.

JUVENILE ROUND TABLE. Third Series. A collection of twenty stories by the foremost writers.

Catholic Circulating Library

Dues, 10c. a Month — A New Book Every Month

NOVELS

12 Copyrighted Novels by the Best Authors

SPECIAL PRICE, $12.00

You get the books at once, and have the use of them while making easy payments

Read explanation of our Circulating Library plan on first page

Library of Novels No. I

THE RULER OF THE KINGDOM. By GRACE KEON. "Will charm any reader."

KIND HEARTS AND CORONETS. By J. HARRISON. "A real, true life history, the kind one could live through and never read it for romance."

IN THE DAYS OF KING HAL. By MARION A. TAGGART. Illustrated. "A tale of the time of Henry V. of England, full of adventure and excitement."

HEARTS OF GOLD. By I. EDHOR. "It is a tale that will leave its reader the better for knowing its heroine, her tenderness and her heart of gold."

THE HEIRESS OF CRONENSTEIN. By COUNTESS HAHN-HAHN. "An exquisite story of life and love, told in touchingly simple words."

THE PILKINGTON HEIR. By ANNA T. SADLIER. "Skill and strength are shown in this story. The plot is well constructed and the characters vividly differentiated."

THE OTHER MISS LISLE. A Catholic novel of South African life. By M. C. MARTIN. A powerful story by a writer of distinct ability.

IDOLS; OR, THE SECRET OF THE RUE CHAUSSEE D'ANTIN. By RAOUL DE NAVERY. "The story is a remarkably clever one; it is well constructed and evinces a master hand."

THE SOGGARTH AROON. By REV. JOSEPH GUINAN, C.C. A capital Irish story.

THE VOCATION OF EDWARD CONWAY. By MAURICE F. EGAN. "This is a novel of modern American life. The scene is laid in a pleasant colony of cultivated people on the banks of the Hudson, not far from West Point."

A WOMAN OF FORTUNE. By CHRISTIAN REID. "That great American Catholic novel for which so much inquiry is made, a story true in its picture of Americans at home and abroad."

PASSING SHADOWS. By ANTHONY YORKE. "A thoroughly charming story. It sparkles from first to last with interesting situations and dialogues that are full of sentiment. There is not a slow page."

12 Copyrighted Novels by the Best Authors

Special New Price, $12.00

$1.00 down, $1.00 a month

Read explanation of our Circulating Library plan on first page.

Library of Novels No. II

THE SENIOR LIEUTENANT'S WAGER, and Other Stories. 30 stories by 30 of the foremost Catholic writers.

A DAUGHTER OF KINGS. By Katharine Tynan Hinkson. "The book is most enjoyable."

THE WAY THAT LED BEYOND. By J. Harrison. "The story does not drag, the plot is well worked out, and the interest endures to the very last page."

CORINNE'S VOW. By Mary T. Waggaman. With 16 full-page illustrations. "There is genuine artistic merit in its plot and life-story. It is full of vitality and action."

THE FATAL BEACON. By F. v. Brackel. "The story is told well and clearly, and has a certain charm that will be found interesting. The principal characters are simple, good-hearted people, and the heroine's high sense of courage impresses itself upon the reader as the tale proceeds."

THE MONK'S PARDON: An Historical Romance of the Time of Philip IV. of Spain. By Raoul de Navery. "A story full of stirring incidents and written in a lively, attractive style."

PERE MONNIER'S WARD. By Walter Lecky. "The characters are lifelike and there is a pathos in the checkered life of the heroine. Pere Monnier is a memory that will linger."

TRUE STORY OF MASTER GERARD. By Anna T. Sadlier. "One of the most thoroughly original and delightful romances ever evolved from the pen of a Catholic writer."

THE UNRAVELING OF A TANGLE. By Marion A. Taggart. With four full-page illustrations. "This story tells of the adventures of a young American girl, who, in order to get possession of a fortune left her by an uncle, whom she had never seen, goes to France."

THAT MAN'S DAUGHTER. By Henry M. Ross. "A well-told story of American life, the scene laid in Boston, New York and California. It is very interesting."

FABIOLA'S SISTER. (A companion volume to Cardinal Wiseman's "Fabiola.") Adapted by A. C. Clarke. "A book to read—a worthy sequel to that masterpiece, 'Fabiola.'"

THE OUTLAW OF CAMARGUE: A Novel. By A. de Lamothe. "A capital novel with plenty of go in it."

12 Copyrighted Novels by the Best Authors

Special Net Price, $12.00

$1.00 down, $1.00 a month

Read explanation of our Circulating Library plan on first page.

Library of Novels No. III

"NOT A JUDGMENT." By Grace Keon. "Beyond doubt the best Catholic novel of the year."

THE RED INN OF ST. LYPHAR. By Anna T. Sadlier. "A story of stirring times in France, when the sturdy Vendeans rose in defence of country and religion."

HER FATHER'S DAUGHTER. By Katharine Tynan Hinkson. "So dramatic and so intensely interesting that the reader will find it difficult to tear himself away from the story."

OUT OF BONDAGE. By M. Holt. "Once his book becomes known it will be read by a great many."

MARCELLA GRACE. By Rosa Mulholland. Mr. Gladstone called this novel *a masterpiece.*

THE CIRCUS-RIDER'S DAUGHTER. By F. v. Brackel. This work has achieved a remarkable success for a Catholic novel, for in less than a year three editions were printed.

CARROLL DARE. By Mary T. Waggaman. Illustrated. "A thrilling story, with the dash of horses and the clash of swords on every side."

DION AND THE SIBYLS. By Miles Keon. "Dion is as brilliantly, as accurately and as elegantly classical, as scholarly in style and diction, as fascinating in plot and as vivid in action as Ben Hur."

HER BLIND FOLLY. By H. M. Ross. A clever story with an interesting and well-managed plot and many striking situations.

MISS ERIN. By M. E. Francis. "A captivating tale of Irish life, redolent of genuine Celtic wit, love and pathos."

MR. BILLY BUTTONS. By Walter Lecky. "The figures who move in rugged grandeur through these pages are as fresh and unspoiled in their way as the good folk of Drumtochty."

CONNOR D'ARCY'S STRUGGLES. By Mrs. W. M. Bertholds. "A story of which the spirit is so fine and the Catholic characters so nobly conceived."

Continuation Library

YOU SUBSCRIBE FOR FOUR NEW NOVELS A YEAR, TO BE MAILED TO YOU AS PUBLISHED, AND RECEIVE BENZIGER'S MAGAZINE FREE.

Each year we publish *four new novels* by the best Catholic authors. These novels are interesting beyond the ordinary—not religious, but Catholic in tone and feeling. They are issued in the best modern style.

We ask you to give us a *standing order* for these novels. The price is $1.25, which will be charged as each volume is issued, and the volume sent postage paid.

As a special inducement for giving us a standing order for the novels, we shall include free a subscription to *Benziger's Magazine*. *Benziger's Magazine* is recognized as the best and handsomest Catholic periodical published, and we are sure will be welcomed in every library. The regular price of the Magazine is $2.00 a year.

Thus for $5.00 a year—paid $1.25 at a time—you will get four good books and receive in addition a year's subscription to *Benziger's Magazine*. The Magazine will be continued from year to year, as long as the standing order for the novels is in force, which will be till countermanded.

THE FAMOUS
ROUND TABLE SERIES

4 VOLUMES, $6.00
50 CENTS DOWN; 50 CENTS A MONTH

On payment of 50 cents you get the books and a free subscription to Benziger's Magazine

The Greatest Stories by the foremost Catholic Writers in the World

With Portraits of the Authors, Sketches of their Lives, and a List of their Works. *Four esquisite volumes,* containing the masterpieces of 86 of the foremost writers of AMERICA, ENGLAND, IRELAND, GERMANY, AND FRANCE. Each story complete. Open any volume at random and you will find a great story to entertain you.

SPECIAL OFFER

In order to place this fine collection of stories in every home, we make the following special offer: *Send us* 50 *cents* and the four fine volumes will be sent to you immediately. Then you pay 50 cents each month until $6.00 has been paid.

LIBRARY OF
SHORT STORIES

BY A BRILLIANT ARRAY OF CATHOLIC AUTHORS
ORIGINAL STORIES BY 33 WRITERS

Four Handsome Volumes and Benziger's Magazine for a Year at the Special Price of $5.00

50 CENTS DOWN; 50 CENTS A MONTH

You get the books at once, and have the use of them while making easy payments. Send us only 50 cents, and we will forward the books at once; 50 cents entitles you to immediate possession. No further payment need be made for a month; afterwards you pay 50 cents a month.

STORIES BY

Anna T. Sadlier	Grace Keon	Rev. T. J. Livingstone, S.J.
Mary E. Mannix	Louisa Emily Dobrée	Marion Ames Taggart
Mary T. Waggaman	Theo. Gift	Maurice Francis Egan
Jerome Harte	Margaret E. Jordan	Mary F. Nixon-Roulet
Mary G. Bonesteel	Agnes M. Rowe	Mrs. Francis Chadwick
Magdalen Rock	Julia C. Walsh	Catherine L. Meagher
Eugenie Uhlrich	Madge Mannix	Anna Blanche McGill
Alice Richardson	Leigh Gordon Giltner	Mary Catherine Crowley
Katharine Jenkins	Eleanor C. Donnelly	Katherine Tynan-Hinkson
Mary Boyle O'Reilly	Teresa Stanton	Sallie Margaret O'Malley
Clara Mulholland	H. J. Carroll	Emma Howard Wight

900 PAGES   500 ILLUSTRATIONS

A GREAT OFFER

THE LIFE OF OUR LORD
══ AND ══
SAVIOUR JESUS CHRIST

AND OF HIS VIRGIN MOTHER MARY

FROM THE ORIGINAL OF

L. C. BUSINGER, LL.D.

BY

Rev. RICHARD BRENNAN, LL.D.

Quarto, half morocco, full gilt side, gilt edges, 900 pages, 500 illustrations in the text and 32 full-page illustrations by

M. FEUERSTEIN

PRICE, ... NET $10.00

EASY PAYMENT PLAN
$1.00 DOWN, $1.00 A MONTH

Mail $1.00 to-day and the book will be shipped to you immediately. Then you pay $1.00 a month till $10.00 is paid.

    This is not only a Life of Christ and of His Blessed Mother, but also a carefully condensed history of God's Church from Adam to the end of the world in type, prophecy and fulfilment, it contains a popular dogmatic theology and a real catechism of perseverance, filled with spiritual food for the soul.

The Best Stories and Articles   Over 1000 Illustrations a Year

BENZIGER'S MAGAZINE

The Popular Catholic Family Monthly

Recommended by 70 Archbishops and Bishops of the United States

SUBSCRIPTION, $2.00 A YEAR

What Benziger's Magazine gives its Readers:

Fifty complete stories by the best writers—equal to a book of 300 pages selling at $1.25.

Three complete novels of absorbing interest—equal to three books selling at $1.25 each.

Over 1000 beautiful illustrations.

Twenty-five large reproductions of celebrated paintings.

Twenty articles—equal to a book of 150 pages—on travel and adventure; on the manners, customs and home-life of peoples; on the haunts and habits of animal life, etc.

Twenty articles—equal to a book of 150 pages—on our country: historic events, times, places, important industries.

Twenty articles—equal to a book of 150 pages—on the fine arts: celebrated artists and their paintings, sculpture, music, etc., and nature studies.

Twelve pages of games and amusements for in and out of doors.

Fifty pages of fashions, fads and fancies, gathered at home and abroad, helpful hints for home workers, household column, cooking receipts, etc.

"Current Events," the important happenings over the whole world, described with pen and pictures.

Prize competitions, in which valuable prizes are offered.

This is what is given in a Single Year of Benziger's Magazine

Send $2.00 now and become a subscriber to the best and handsomest Catholic Magazine published.

BENZIGER BROTHERS

NEW YORK:	CINCINNATI:	CHICAGO:
36-38 Barclay Street.	343 Main Street.	211-213 Madison Street.

www.ingramcontent.com/pod-product-compliance
Lightning Source LLC
Chambersburg PA
CBHW030811230426
43667CB00008B/1166